Two Sisters & a Brain Tumour

a Memoir

EMILY J. MAURITS

D.O.L.L.

Daughters of Love & Light
www.daughtersofloveandlight.com
Adelaide, South Australia
admin@daughtersofloveandlight.com

© Emily J. Maurits 2021

ISBN: 9780645252705

All rights reserved. Except for private study, research, criticism or reviews, as permitted under the Copyright Act, no part of this book may be reproduced, stored in a retrieval system, or transmitted in any form or by any means without prior written permission. Enquiries should be made to the publisher.

Scripture quotations marked (NIV) are taken from the Holy Bible, New International Version®, NIV®. Copyright © 1973, 1978, 1984, 2011 by Biblica, Inc.™ Used by permission of Zondervan. All rights reserved worldwide. www.zondervan.com The "NIV" and "New International Version" are trademarks registered in the United States Patent and Trademark Office by Biblica, Inc.™

O Father my Father (Robin Mann, 1973). Used with permission. *Amazing Grace* (John Newton), *My Orders* (Agnes Ethelwyn Wetherald), *O the deep, deep love of Jesus* (Trevor Francis), and other cited works in the public domain.

Publisher's Note: This is a work of non-fiction. Names of persons have been changed or used with permission.

Cataloguing-in-Publications entry is available from the National Library of Australia http:/catalogue.nla.gov.au

First edition published 2021

Dedication

To Jay.
You have been given to me twice over,
and I am forever grateful.

Foreword

In 2015 my sister Jasmine was diagnosed with a large craniopharyngioma.

This benign brain tumour suppressed the production of hormones, while causing fatigue and loss of vision. She spent three months in hospital and underwent nine brain surgeries and three lumbar drain placements.

During this time I kept two separate diaries. While many of the names and descriptions of individuals apart from my immediate family have been changed, I have attempted to make the following account as accurate as possible.

In instances where conversations or thoughts cannot be accurately recovered, I have ensured they are representative of similar conversations or thoughts.

PART ONE

Chapter One: Just a Normal MRI

You can read an x-ray and tell someone they've broken their wrist. You can glance at a CT and tell someone they may have kidney stones. You can't study an MRI and tell someone they have a brain tumour. Even if it's true.

I haven't quite finished my final year of radiography, but I know this much.

'Sorry, I'm going to have to go – I've got a few missed calls from my mum, and my sister had an appointment today so they might be important.' I wave goodbye to my uni friends outside the lecture hall and squint at my phone screen. Blue shapes hop out of the edges of my vision. I blink and wait for my eyes to adjust to the slanting sun after the artificial darkness. Then I turn off the pathway and walk across the grass until I reach the privacy of the straggly trees near the campus fence.

Messages received (3). Mum:

Ring me.

Just got home.

Can you ring me?

 I juggle my laptop to my other arm and hit *call*. Students sweep by me towards the bus stop, until a group with a football congregates in the middle of the path and begins an impromptu game. Physio students, the ball tells me, as the other students navigate the obstacle with good grace. This is the health science campus, isolated from the politics of the main university site, and renowned for its general friendliness. A smile can't do much in the face of illness, I know from experience, but I'm proud that we try.
 Beneath the chatter a reverberating chorus of cicadas begins, rising from the bushes which line the tall wire fence. I scratch a mosquito bite. 'Hello? It's me. What's wro—'
 'Emily! One second, I just need to put the washing on… How are you?'
 'Good. What's wrong? I'm about to leave…' I glance at my watch, phone still clamped to my ear. I don't want

to miss the connecting bus and have to walk the final forty minutes of my commute. *Hurry up Mum,* I urge silently.

'Jasmine had her MRI today. You know, the one the doctor—'

'I know.'

'Anyway, they gave us a copy of the MRI as soon as it was over. All the pictures! Is that normal?'

I shrug, and almost drop the phone. 'I don't know. So there's no report yet?'

'No, just the pictures, and Emily, I think she has something.'

'Has something? Has *what?*' A brain? Unexpected, certainly, but hardly worth a phone call or a missed bus. I begin to walk towards the campus gates.

'I don't know, I can't read it properly. I just looked at the brain and there's something there, and I thought you'd be able to read it. When are you home?'

'As soon as I get on the bus.' I allow exasperation to slink into my words. 'You can't get worried, Mum, it's probably normal. MRI scans look different to CTs and x-rays, you know…'

'But it's bright. There's a bright lump in the middle. Is that normal?'

'I don't know! They use different contrast to highlight different things, I'm sure it's just a normal scan. I'll have a look when I get home, okay?' I breathe in.

'Mum, please don't worry. MRIs can look funny sometimes, but it'll be fine, okay?'

'*Okay!*' Mum registers my frustration. 'Okay. See you soon.'

I shove my phone into my satchel and jog out from the shadows of the trees. My bus appears on the horizon. Mum is not the worried type. She does not generally ring me in a panic. I reach the road. Cars and lorries zoom by. They really need a pedestrian crossing here. The bus trundles to a stop and the bus shelter empties. I crane my neck left and right. Should I run for it? *Please let me through,* I beg the passing cars. They don't stop. The bus huffs and groans, then jerks forward and onward, leaving me behind on the opposite side of the road.

There can't be anything wrong with Jasmine's MRI if I can do something as normal as miss my bus. Mum doesn't know how to read MRIs. I don't even know how to read them yet! A ute lets me through, and I wave a 'thanks-mate!' and run across the road, bag thudding against my hip.

On the other side I wonder why I bothered. It's twenty minutes until the next bus and I'm the only one at the stop. The back of the graffitied shelter rubs against the high wall of Rookwood Cemetery. It's the largest burial ground in the southern hemisphere, according to Wikipedia. It's a genuine paradox, of the everyday variety: a health science campus, dedicated to saving lives, only a short sprint from an overgrown, sprawling reminder of death.

Annoying little sisters don't have 'things in their brains'. The very idea eclipses everyday realities – even everyday paradoxes – and lands in the realm of impossibility. I relax on the metal bench. The MRI will be normal.

It has to be.

'Hey.' I dump my laptop and bag on the dining room floor beneath the calendar overflowing with Mum's specialist appointments, and, more recently, my sister's. There's a big white envelope on the phone table. 'Is this it?' Mum's stirring a saucepan on the stove. 'And where's Jay?' I turn, as though expecting to find the answer printed on the back of her neck.

'Upstairs. She was tired and I said she should have a lie down before dinner.' Mum comes over. 'What do you see?'

'Can't I even get a drink first?' I grumble, more to inject reality into the situation than because I'm thirsty. I don't like this frowning, worried person. I want pre-MRI Mum back.

Pulling a chair out at the dining table I yank the films from their bag. Static causes the sheets to cling together and I'm forced to peel them apart one by one. It takes a good minute, but Mum doesn't waver from her vigil at my shoulder. I shrug away and flip the blue-tinged film to orientate it correctly. Where are the axial views? I suppose I should start there. Here we go. 'Top of head, sutures, ventricles—'

'There! Do you see it?' Mum jabs a finger from behind.

If 'it' was a white, bright (hyperdense, my university lecturer supplies in my ear), round mass in the centre of Jasmine's brain behind her nose, then yes, I see it. All too well.

For goodness sakes. 'Mum, it could be anything! It's probably normal in this scan phase. Or, at the very least, it's a normal variant. Brains always look odd on MRIs, this doesn't mean she has a *tumour!*'

'Shh!' Mum gestures upstairs to Jasmine's bedroom. 'Keep your voice down! She hasn't seen the pictures.' Mum walks over to the desktop computer in the corner. 'I Googled what a brain MRI should look like, and none of the pictures have that! Then I Googled what it *could* be, and it sounds like a large pituitary adenoma. The website said you have to have brain surgery and -'

'Mum! You *know* you can't trust Google! You know that!'

'Shh! Look!'

She pulls me over to the screen. I shake off her clawing hand and glance at the webpages. I completely expect to find URLS like ilovebraintumours.com or greenteacuresall.net, but the pages seem reputable. I've trained Mum well, and it's about to be my downfall. 'Mum, it could be anything. Just because it looks like a brain tumour doesn't mean it is. This is why they tell people not to read their reports without a doctor. It could be a benign cyst, it could be—'

'But it doesn't look like a cyst,' Mum protests. Apparently, she's a qualified neuroradiologist. I wish I could achieve that in a single afternoon.

'I Googled that too,' she continues, 'and pituitary tumours can make someone fatigued, it says, and cause loss of vision, *and* interrupt hormone production. They're normally found before the child reaches puberty, but if not they can cause stunted growth due to lack of hormones.'

Jasmine's underactive thyroid, below average height, sudden new glasses prescription, and excessive tiredness hang between us, spectres pointing to a devastating end.

Not on my watch. 'Mum, please,' I beg. 'We don't know. We don't know anything. Bodies are complex, MRIs are hard to read. Even if she does have this tumour, we can't do anything about it until the doctor tells us. There's no point in worrying or stressing about it. Besides, think how rare it must be. How could *Jasmine* have a *brain tumour?*'

It's this last appeal to the inviolable script of our lower-middle-class lives which finally relaxes the wrinkles above Mum's eyes. 'You're right,' she admits. 'But still, it would explain a lot of her symptoms…'

'Did the radiographer say anything when she gave you the pictures?'

'She asked if our doctor's appointment was soon.'

Fiddlesticks. That phrase is classic professional code for *I am concerned.* I begin putting the films back in their bag. There's a lot of them and they're heavy and slippery now I actually want them to be clingy. The corners all bear the same identification tag in Times New Roman: JASMINE S. MAURITS 16 YEAR OLD FEMALE. Too young to have a brain tumour. 'When is it?'

'Tuesday,' Mum mouths as footsteps sound above us. Jasmine. The front door crashes. Dad's home. The stovetop emits a curdling noise.

I 'switch users' on the computer and tuck the films away. If Mum's going to Google things like this, I really need to teach her how to open an *incognito* tab. The web pages slide away and normality returns.

My bedroom carpet nuzzles against my bare legs, scratchy and hot. The lights have been off for a while, but sleep won't come. The MRI *was* normal, wasn't it? My earlier, desperate reassurances cycle and recycle before me: flimsy words, terror masquerading as truth.

I have no desire to re-open Google on my phone and dig up more information. What's the point? If Mum's correct, there will be plenty of time to worry in the future – why start now over a white spot on a scan I can't read, which is probably not a tumour?

I suspect it is.

Bringing my knees up is the only way I can squash the rubbery jelly-fish lurking in my stomach, pressing on my chest, sending electric currents up my neck. I rest my chin on my kneecaps and my short-short hair barely flops down to my eyebrows.

I shaved it for Mum's type 1 diabetes a few months ago, and people assumed I was shaving for cancer. Of course not. Cancer and tumours are things that everyone else gets. Teachers at school, friends of friends, workmates' aunties – those sorts of people are allowed to grow tumours and get cancer. Not my sister.

It's a mistake, isn't it God? The MRI... the symptoms... But they match up so well! *Idiot.* Don't jump to conclusions. How can someone else in my family have medical issues? What happens when you have a tumour?

Will she die?

In my small room surrounded by thick, clammy silence, I believe she can. Every word Mum spoke, every suggestion Google planted feels far more real now in the dark epicentre of the night than they did at 5.30 pm this afternoon. I try and push the question away, but it returns like an annoying computer pop-up. Tumour – brain – death – death – death –

I wish I could believe the comfort I offered Mum, but my own mind is not that obliging. Instead I close my eyes and launch myself into another realm, a realm no less real than the one breaking down around me. I see and create a picture instantaneously: Jasmine, cradled in a pair of ginormous hands. And in this realm beyond physics, I know they are God's hands and they will not let her fall.

I hope. *Don't let her die. Don't let her die.* My fervent chant drags me back into my own reality, and then back further, back in time…

'Have you – have you been reading anything in the Bible lately?' The question prickles unnaturally on my tongue. Too stilted, too formal – yet it's the only way I know to broach the topic of What Matters Most to Me. Experience whispers that I'm already doomed.

Jasmine stares into the distance. 'Um, we're reading Luke at school.'

'Yeah? What're you learning?'

'I dunno.' She shrugs. 'Stuff.'

'About Jesus?' I sound sweet and I hate it. But how else am I to ask?

'Obviously.'

I grab a frustrated sigh just before it escapes. 'How about by yourself?'

'Why're you asking all these questions?'

'Because I want to.' Because you never talk about anything real. Because I want to know if Jesus means anything to you. Because I would do anything for us to share this one thing.

'You're not my mum.' We walk along the wide main road. Brown leaf stains mar the white concrete. Gum nuts crunch underfoot. The smell of eucalyptus burrows up my nostrils.

'I never said I was.' I breathe in. 'I'm just trying to talk to you! You never talk.'

She makes a face. 'We're talking now!'

'Not about anything important!'

'Stop trying to be better than me! You're so perfect.'

'I. Am. Not. Perfect.' I'd sort of like to strangle her. Sort of really like to. I growl instead and I'm not sure it's much of an improvement.

'Sure.' She rolls her eyes. 'I'm tired. Can we go home now?'

I glare at her spindly legs and baby-smooth face. *Lord, I can't make her love you. I've tried everything. You have to do this. Make her love You more than anything. Please. Whatever it takes.*

Do it.

In the present I shuffle to relieve the cramps in my legs. May as well go back to bed. I pull my sheets to my chin and stare at the ceiling. Try as I might, I can't seem to re-enter the realm where Jasmine is okay. Time buckles and stretches. I feel as though I've been lying here forever, and as the night curves around me like a burial chamber around a body, I wonder if there are certain prayers which should never, *ever,* be prayed.

Chapter Two: How Many Tears is a Brain Tumour Worth?

When Jasmine was one year old she threw a temper tantrum. I tried to comfort her and she bit my knee. It's a funny story I like to tell for sympathy and giggles. It's not a story which will help me now, because there's nothing remotely funny about tonight.

I can hear her screams through the wall. Fury. Frustration. Fear. A loud thump like something has been pushed against the plaster, or she's thrown herself down on her bed. It is official. She has a brain tumour and it's big.

You'd think I wouldn't be too surprised, after the MRI. I am. It's like watching *Hamlet*. Denmark's devastation is foreshadowed again and again, from scene one onwards, but when it happens it's still a tragedy. It's still shocking and wrong. Perhaps a brain tumour is like that. An event which not only rends the curtain of normality, but yanks the cloth from the curtain rings as well.

Jasmine doesn't cry for long, all things considered. How many tears are a brain tumour worth? Who would dare decide? Who has the courage and patience to measure?

I won't go into her room. To do so would imply that her reaction is too big, that it needs to be managed, controlled, contained… If you have a brain tumour, *I* decide, you are allowed all the tears in the world. It doesn't matter if you are sixteen, and far too old to be throwing things. Normal rules do not apply here. *How to Respond to a Brain Tumour: A Manual in 7 Steps* does not exist.

If a temper tantrum is her response, well, does it matter? There are worse ways of responding. Envy prickles tightly in my calves. Does this apparent permission to grieve in socially unacceptable ways extend to family members as well? I suspect not.

Leaning back against the corner of my desk, I let my head bump uncomfortably against the wooden drawer knobs. My feet stretch out on the carpet. Allowing myself to be dwarfed by the bedroom furniture is the most comfort I can obtain right now. The closest I can get to being held. Downstairs Mum and Dad will be talking in terse, serious voices. I do not want to join them. I don't want to know any more; I don't want to hear the facts; and most of all I don't want to talk about how bad it will be.

If the hospital-issued information booklet was supposed to be encouraging, they gave us the wrong one.

Any day now life as I know it is going to crash to the ground around me. I shiver like a kid on the edge of a pool in the pale light of a winter morning. Before long the whistle will blow and I will have to jump in. If I'm not ready, I'll be pushed.

I pick up my journal and pen from the carpet. I need to be prepared. I need to make plans. Not many get the opportunity to stand on the cold tiles at the edge of the water, so the least I can do is make sure I have my floaties on.

Lord, please let this time be different...

Knock, knock.

'Mmm?'

The door opens. Dad's head appears, cheeks newly shaven. 'We're not going out to lunch, did you hear?'

'Yes.' I don't look up from the corner of my bedroom. I've curled myself between my desk and bookshelf. Ginormous hands.

'Mum's not well.'

'I know.' I drag out the vowel. This is old news.

His head retreats and then it is back, returning with its body to stand in my doorway. 'Are you okay?'

'Yes!'

'Okay.' Dad disappears and then he's back. Again. Why won't he just leave? 'We'll go another time—'

'It's fine! I don't care!' I raise the book on my lap, 'I'm busy reading anyway.'

He believes me and leaves. It doesn't feel as good as I expected. 'Close the door!' I call… and it clicks closed.

I shut my eyes, clenching my lids together. You'd need a crowbar to pry them apart. I don't care – I don't care – I don't care – The book slips to the floor. My legs are twisted uncomfortably and there's a familiar burning behind my eyes. Don't cry – don't cry – It's your own stupid fault, Emily. You let yourself get excited.

There's a clothes button on my bookshelf, and I pick it up. I need distraction. I'll take anything… I won't cry. I won't be disappointed. I'm too old for either of those things. Besides, it might make Mum feel worse than her migraine is already doing, and I won't be part of that. Only an idiot would pretend their disappointment is equal to someone else's pain.

I roll the blue, transparent disc between my fingers. I push down. Firmer. Firmer, until there's a red dent in my thumb pad. The button is from my pyjamas. I ripped it off myself, while asleep, and woke up with it in my hand. There's a tiny bit of fabric still attached. I don't actually care about the lunch. I mean, we go out for a meal maybe once a year, for a big birthday or an anniversary, so it would have been nice.

But it's the principle of the matter. Another thing God has taken from me. Another disappointment. When will it stop hurting? It's my own fault that I still hope. You'd think I'd have learnt by now. I look at the button, impressed by my somnolent strength. Strength is good. Anger is good. Much better than grief and confusion and loneliness.

Even so... I sort of wish I could swap places with Jay. Happy-go-Lucky Jay who, unashamed to cry, has reaped the consolation of playing a board game with Dad, and thus restored balance to her world. Why can't I be like her? Why do I feel so much?

I throw the button as hard as I can. It tinkles against my bookshelf and falls to the floor. I draw my disappointment towards me in exchange, and close my eyes. In a minute I will pick up my book again and try and forget. In a minute I will go downstairs and try and be a decent human being. In a minute I will behave my age.

But for sixty whole seconds I will nurse my disappointment until it turns to bitterness. *Please Lord, I know it's wrong, but just let me have this. What's a minute after all?*

I open my eyes and breathe out. I'm back at the edge of the 'pool', and I don't want that minute anymore. *Lord, I don't want this all to be in vain. Bring good out of this. Save Jasmine. Save us all.*

Picking up my pen, I begin my To Do list. I need to talk to someone. However painful it is, I need to share my grief. Not because it's easy or will make me feel better, but because it will help me heal. And if I'm not at least partly together how can I support Jasmine? My parents? I know this because I got it wrong the first time around. I didn't talk for years about how painful I found Mum's illnesses and I suffered the consequences. Sadness. Loneliness. Shame.

God is powerful but He's also good. It's taken me a long time to believe the latter. How can a good God allow sick parents and brain tumours? I don't pretend to understand, but my lack of comprehension does not change who God is. I believe that, as firmly as I believe that I don't have it all together, that I can't do this.

There's no 'I just need to be stronger' anymore. Pulling off buttons and hiding tears does not prove anything except that I'm a restless sleeper and afraid of being vulnerable. For the first time in my life I'm entering disaster with my eyes wide open… and I'm terrified. I'm not the moody teenager I once was, but neither am I equipped for this. Whatever 'this' is.

How do I say the words?

DIARY EXCERPT
August 30, 2015

My sister has a brain tumour.

I've always hated euphemisms. Don't tell me my grandmother passed away. Nothing can soften the blow, so at least acknowledge my grief and tell me that she died. But somehow, I would prefer to say, 'my sister has a tumour in her brain'. The phrase 'brain tumour' is ominous.

But it's more than merely a matter of personal fear. The term is a dramatic one, and carries an enormous load of misconceptions and beliefs. It feels wrong to tell people that. As if I'm exaggerating, or using it for shock effect, or worse, for sympathy.

Besides, I'm so mindful, so acutely aware, of the situation the phrase places people in. The sanitised, hospital wall it places them against. There's no escape, no pre-prepared social niceties to combat that phrase. It's real and unforgiving, and I don't want to place people into that situation merely to make myself feel better.

And yet, it makes me feel like a traitor to her very real anguish and suffering to use words that are any less. Words are so cheap, and at the same time so hard. How do I stay true to her reality – to my reality – in a way that is kind and accessible? Is there a way?

If so, I haven't found it. All my imagined conversations take place in a vacuum, in a place sharply separated from the miasmas of life. But this will not always be the case. And how do I find a situation, an atmosphere, a reality, that can couch the words 'brain tumour'? Is there one?

Every place seems wrong. And so I carry around the knowledge and the reality, and it weighs me down, and there's no appropriate context to let it go. I feel like every conversation where It is not mentioned is a lie, like I'm propping up a façade and pointing everyone towards it, while with the other hand I clench the tumour so hard I can't breathe. The lie of omission, they say, is of equal weight to the lie of commission.

Chapter Three: The Kettle Explodes

'Hi?' I let myself in; the door is unlocked. My kettle of unspoken words hisses dangerously. I don't have long now. A few steps take me down the narrow hallway and tumbling into the sunny kitchen. The journey is short and instantly rewarding. I doubt my coming conversation will be. *Help me, Lord.*

'Good to see you, friend.' Maria looks up and smiles, a toddler on the floor by her feet.

'Likewise.' I allow myself one smile, intuiting that it's too early in the conversation to tear the world apart. And then, so I don't have to meet her eyes, I squat on the laminate. 'Hey, Hope, what're you doin'?'

The blonde head wiggles as she decides whether to answer. It's nice to focus solely on someone else. All week I've shied from anything beyond shallow niceties, afraid people will read the truth in my eyes and the falsehood in my words. Three-year-olds don't notice these things. Or if they do, they trust the grown-ups to take care of it.

'C'mon Hope, tell Emily what you're drawing.'

'A sun,' the blonde head mumbles, and then her courage fails and she retreats to her mother's side beneath a storm of rustling paper.

'How are you?' Maria picks Hope up and deposits her in the highchair, then comes over. We hug.

'I'm okay.' The lie is worn and tired, but oh so comfortable. Habitual too, because I spent the walk over preparing myself to answer truthfully, and it slipped out all the same. 'Well, sort of. Not really.' The admission edges out with all the willingness of three tonne blocks of concrete.

'What's wrong?'

'Can we walk?'

'Peter!' Maria scoops up three nectarines from the cluttered kitchen counter with one hand and checks the saucepan on her stove with the other. Her husband appears, so much like her they could have been blood relations. Tall, dark, slim. The blonde child is an odd, but somehow perfect, contrast.

'Emily.' He smiles. 'How are you?'

It's the question of the day. I'm not answering a second time. Maria hands me a piece of fruit and the action offers me a refuge from which I mumble, 'I'm okay.'

If Peter were a uni friend he'd stop, startled, and ask why I am just 'okay' and not 'good' – as though 'good' is our right, or even our default state – but he's my minister and his kitchen table has absorbed its fair share of sighs and tears. He simply nods. Perhaps he can hear the whistling of my kettle of secrets. It's hit boiling point. 'And how's your sister? Your mum mentioned after church a few weeks ago that she was having some tests?'

'She did?' I thought the tests were our house's current elephant in residence. The skeleton in our closet. Evidently not. 'She's not so good.' I can feel my face going soft, on the verge of melting like... well, not wax. Something softer, something with the power to set off an unstoppable reaction. A reaction which mustn't happen here. My kettle begins to rattle.

They don't let the silence become awkward. In less than fifteen minutes Hope is strapped into a pram with a hat on her head, clutching a mushy nectarine with all ten fingers. 'You can turn the stove off when the pot boils!' calls Maria as we head towards the door. Her husband waves an acknowledgement from the kitchen, curlicues of mist dancing above his cup of tea. I wish my stove had an off switch.

Conversation about children and weather and how long until I graduate take us across the road and halfway down the winding path of the bushland reserve. It's a beautiful day. Clear sky, hot sun. Summer has arrived in the final month of winter and I'm glad I thought to bring a hat. We follow the path, the bulges in my friend's biceps testifying to the steepness of the decline. If the pram escapes her grip only cracked concrete and tangled scrubland will cushion its descent.

'Listen, Hope! Water. Shall we splash in it?'

I want to smile at the tinkling noise, such a rare sound against a bush backdrop, but I've used up my day's quota.

'I like it here,' I say, gesturing at the overhanging trees as we yank the pram off the path and onto the rockbed. Maria unbuckles her daughter, and while I *do* like the tiny nature reserve tucked behind the strip of houses and the way the trees create a private oasis in this particular spot, I'm also suddenly aware that perhaps I've just used up my small talk quota too. Is tragedy always so stingy? Hamlet certainly found a lot to say.

Jasmine and I discovered a red-bellied black snake lying on these rocks a few weeks ago, sunning itself beside the trickling stream. Not believing in premonitions, spotting the serpent had given me a delicious tingle of fear. That's how Death is supposed to come, encased in slothful, opalescent scales, both beautiful and avoidable. Already the memory is a nostalgic treasure. Jay and I don't walk together anymore.

'Jasmine had the tests and they did a brain MRI and they found a brain tumour and it's big.' My kettle explodes without warning and the words boil out. I stare at the tiny blonde-haired toddler squatting on the water-stained rock. 'They're going to operate and she's lost her peripheral vision and that's why she wasn't developing and they said it has probably been growing since birth...' I take a breath and I meet my friend's eyes.

Horror. Sadness. '*Oh Emily.*'

'And I know it could be worse, and I know she will probably live and be okay and it's good they can treat it but I'm *sad*.' And I hadn't realised it until now.

'*Ohh.*' It's such an expressive noise. Is that what agony sounds like? Is that what I should be feeling? I cry as I wait for Maria to speak, and the action brings no relief at all. 'Hope, stop! Careful!' Maternal instinct eclipses her sympathy, and for one whole second I hate the tiny child trying to jump on slippery ground. 'Play over here, see. You can splash like this, Hope, but don't jump.'

Maybe it's two seconds.

'Oh, my friend.' Maria is back. 'How awful. That's… I don't know what to say.'

I've never seen her eyes so sad, and we have been friends since I was a teenager, right through its giddy highs and devastating lows.

'I'm so, so scared.' Again, I realise it's true as I speak. 'I've never been so scared, and I don't know why because

I'm sure it won't be as bad as it sounds and God will bring something good out of it, but—'

'I know why. It's huge. You're allowed to be scared.'

I cry and she holds me. The air is damp and cool beneath the trees. The sight of running water is refreshing, even if it does come out of a storm drain. After a while I learn you have to cry a very long time for your tears to splatter to the ground. It's almost impossible for them to travel that far. It's not like a Disney movie where one perfectly shaped droplet manages to plop nicely into concentric rings on every conveniently placed puddle.

'Have you been able to pray?'

I watch her tiny child stamp around and wish I could draw some hauntingly beautiful and tragic parallel to my sister, but my heart hurts too much. 'Yes.' I latch onto the single thought my tears have left behind. 'I don't know what to do.'

We sit on the rock, facing the stream. I splinter fragments of whip grass until it can barely be seen against the multi-coloured rock. 'I'm not angry. I thought I would be. Goodness knows I spent enough time being angry over Mum's health when I was little. I thought with this I would be angry all over again.' I know how to deal with anger. I know how to run so fast the tears can't leave my eyes and the shocks from my feet hitting the pavement run all the way up into my hips. I know how to pound the trees in the bush near my house until my fists bleed, and how to scream silently to God until all I see is red.

'But I'm not angry. I know, *I know*, God. I know He is powerful and I know He is good. I'm not angry. Is that wrong?'

'I think,' Maria begins, her eyes on her daughter even as mine fill up once more, 'that it is a sign of maturity. Because your Mum's been sick all your life, you have come to know Jesus in a very real way. You have seen him beside you during suffering. Anger isn't necessarily wrong, and you might be angry later. But it sounds like you've dealt with anger. You've known pain and what it is to watch others in pain. You've moved on from anger.'

I duck my head. 'Anger was easier! Without it I feel like I'm not reacting enough.'

'Do you feel numb?'

'Yes! No! I feel sad and scared. So, so scared,' I repeat, 'and I don't know what to do.'

'I would be scared too.' She's caught my tears, as I used to catch Jay's infectious smiles. They trickle down her nose behind her glasses. Has Mum cried yet? If so, it must be behind bedroom doors, because we are all Putting On a Brave Front.

'If it was Hope I can't imagine how I'd feel...'

The blonde girl is the fruit of a decade of struggle, a living, breathing answer to prayer. This is how God works. He raises velvet flowers in desert places and summons pinpricks of light out of inky darkness. Surely he will do the same for Jasmine? He *must*.

'... it's a huge operation, and the future is so uncertain. What will life look like afterwards? It will never be the same.'

'They said she could get diabetes insipidus from the surgery,' I say. Maria's words remind me of the others I've heard this week. 'It's not diabetes like Mum's type 1 insulin diabetes. It means she'll never be able to retain water inside her body again without medication. It's to do with the pituitary gland. I know it probably won't happen,' I'm not catastrophizing. I'm not! 'but Mum's worried and there's a *chance*. And of course there's...'

Blindness. Disability. Death.

'...*so* much that could go wrong. And even if it doesn't, I'm still scared!' And exhausted. 'What do I do?' I ask for the third time. If anger is hot energy, fear is cold nothingness. And nothingness is too much like not caring. But I care so, *so* much. It's a Gordian's Knot I can't untangle and it makes my stomach hurt.

'Go to Jesus, my friend,' Maria says, so quietly I can barely hear her over the tireless water. 'Take everything to him, like the psalm writers did. It can't be wrong if you bring it to him.' She stands up.

I follow her eyes and see her daughter toddling towards the opening of the storm drain.

'You're allowed to be afraid.' Maria continues, as she watches the blonde child. 'You're allowed to be sad. I love that Jesus says, 'cast all your worries onto me.' He doesn't say, 'don't have worries.' He just says, 'I watch over each sparrow.''

'I want to go about this the right way.' My words sound rough and unpolished after her gentle reassurances. Not at all like a sparrow. More like a galah, a desperately determined galah, shrieking challenges in the face of a raging bushfire. 'If this has to happen,' I affirm, 'I want to cling to Jesus.' It's the only thing I'm sure of – and I am more sure of it than I have been of anything since the MRI.

The trees are casting muddled shadows now and the coolness from the rocks is beginning to leach into the shivering breeze. A magpie calls across the reserve. My friend begins to buckle Hope into her pram.

'By the way, it's a secret.' It's the least we can do. We can't take away Jasmine's tumour, but we can respect her privacy, and let her tell her own story, in her own time, in her own way.

Maria turns to face me.

'You're the third person I've told,' I blurt, 'and it's the first time I've actually cried.'

Can God's presence be enough?

DIARY EXCERPT
September 5, 2015

I am at peace.

Not in a happy way. Not in a 'the world is brilliant' sort of way. There are decisions I have to make, and sadness I have to feel, and do feel. There are hard conversations I must have, and relationships I must traverse. There are many ways I have to grow, and there's even a sort of unsettled feeling in my stomach which has been there a lot lately. So many unknowns. But more than that, so much sacrifice.

Does anyone actually like to sacrifice? Or being forced into positions where they have to choose to be selfless? I wish I delighted in following in my Jesus' footsteps in such a way. Perhaps someday. Please Lord… But meanwhile I am flooded with this strange sense of peace.

Because come hell or high water, my God is… there.

…It doesn't mean victory, and it definitely doesn't mean happiness. But it does mean constancy. It does mean that God is behind me, in front of me, all around me, as St. Patrick's prayer goes. It means that my life is being drawn inexorably towards a single point; it means that it will culminate, not in the cross, but in the resurrection.

...So I sit, and by God's mercy, God's presence is enough.

Chapter Four: Running Away From Church

'You're not coming to church?'

Jasmine turns to face the wall. 'No.'

'Why not?' I know why.

'I'm not going!'

'Okay, okay,' I raise my hands. Suck in a breath. Dare to lean against the hinges of her bedroom door. 'Don't you think... don't you think you *should*?' I've never been more conscious that I ought to be A Role Model. I'm four years older after all, even if I am brain tumour free.

She snorts. Wet, muffled, wild.

'Sometimes we have to do things we're afraid of—'

'Muuuummm! Emily's trying to force me to go to church!'

Mum comes out of the bathroom door behind me. I spin around, already planning my defence. It's yet another unspoken rule which has arisen since the diagnosis: don't oppose the girl with the brain tumour. I'm not sure if it's a house rule or a universal one.

'Emily, Jasmine's got a sore throat, remember? She can't risk it getting worse before the operation.'

'I know, I know. I just thought...' I trail off. If *I* were Jasmine, I would go to church. I wouldn't hide away, afraid of awkward questions and pitying glances. Instead I would stick out my chin and embody one of the 'plucky young children' from my childhood readers. It would only be fair. They raised me, moulded me, created me in their likeness during those endless summers when Mum was too sick to leave the house six days out of seven and my favourite hours in the week were those after each long-anticipated library visit. They were my friends, my role models and my escape. It would be rude to abandon them now.

I sit in the car and stare holes into the windscreen as bush flashes by on one side and houses on the other. *You're making this far more momentous than it really is, Emily. What are you, some martyr on your way to certain death?* No, that's Jasmine. *Lord, don't let me make it about myself.*

The drive takes four minutes. In four minutes our vow of silence will be over. Everyone will be astonished, everyone will have questions, everyone will pity...

'The church congregation needs to know so they can pray.' That was Dad's argument. Words are not his strong point, but they didn't have to be. His desperation — not safely contained in his eyes but superimposed over his entire being - was enough. I've never seen anything like it. Not when his father died, not when my childhood friend passed away at the age of six. Not until now.

'You can't keep it a secret forever.' Mum was persuasive, no-nonsense. 'It's easier this way. Do you really want to have to tell all your friends individually?'

Together they presented a united front. Jasmine's rebuttal began with a grumbled 'not all my friends are at church,' and ended in violent tears and a slammed bedroom door. I proofread an email to the church congregation, and we hit 'send' together, Dad, Mum and I. Three equals. Three parents. One month before I turn twenty-one.

I'm not sure if the hugs and tears and 'I can't believe it!'s make the situation better or worse. At least there's not much time for them before the band starts keying up. I stare more holes during the announcement from the pulpit, this time into the plastic seat in front of me. If I practise ocular-pyrotechnics I don't have to meet the disturbed and grieving glances radiating from the people sitting around us.

Suddenly making it 'not about me' is very hard. It's *my* eyes that are filling with tears, *my* chin that is trying to turn to jelly, and *my* body that I must control. I wish I were at home with Jasmine. But no, I chose to be brave.

We begin to sing. By 'we' I mean the congregation. By 'we' I mean everyone whose sister is brain tumour free. By 'we' I mean not me.

I know my vocal cords will commit treason if I attempt to use them. Instead I mash my nails into my palms, stiffen my legs, and mouth the lyrics. My shoulders are so stiff you would break your fingers trying to give me a massage. Injecting them with cement is the only way I can stop my entire body falling apart.

My sister has a brain tumour. All these people believe it so it must be true. All these people are shocked so it must be shocking…It's actually a big thing, their eyes tell me, a very big thing, a momentous thing. I stoop down and pull a tissue from my bag as unobtrusively as possible. My shoulders don't lose their starch. My chin does. The song swelling around me throws promises like stones.

You can pray during tough times.

I can't even mouth the lyrics. My lips are wobbling too much.

You can pray as you wait for a happy ending.

What if there's no happy ending for me, for Jay?

What if I wait and it never comes?

You can sing, because God is God whatever happens.

If Jay dies, I think I might die too. There will be no singing then.

Good will come.

Will it? All at once, my tissue is overcome, and so am I. 'I have to go.' I lean against Mum's bony shoulder, seconds away from falling to the floor and wailing like a child. 'I can't stop.'

'Do you want me to come?' Her face softens as empathy dials her age from fifty-eight to thirty.

I was supposed to be brave for her. 'No. I just need to go.' I push past Dad, make it out of the row of chairs, and for a second am blinded by a visage of singing, open mouths and staring eyes. Then it dissolves, but not as much as I'd like. I flee down the aisle to the back door and pull it open. I don't try and do it quietly. Reverence is a luxury I can't afford. The band plays on. People sing on. With a nudge of a handle I shut it all out.

'Are you okay?' A young mum is nursing on the foyer couch. She gets to her feet and comes towards me. Concern and sympathy cling tightly to her eyes. If I shake my head I will have a shoulder to lean on and a person to cry with and wise counsel as well.

'Yes, I just need to...' I charge past her and out the main door. Fresh air. I suck it in. Sweeping trees, birds, a tree-bark strewn car park. My soldier shoulders finally fall, and I run.

Across the street, a man's mowing his front lawn. I can picture him at the dinner table tonight, shaking his head. 'Saw a girl running out of the church over the road this morning. Face all blotchy. Crying. Goodness knows what they do in that place.'

His wife, doubtfully: 'Was she wearing a long dress?'

He rubs his sunburnt neck. 'No, jeans I think.' He scratches. 'Pants, at any rate.'

She nods, relieved. Not a cult then. 'Where'd she go?'

Turning back to his dinner, already tasting the cool beer waiting in the refrigerator. 'Down the hill, towards the bush.'

As fast as I possibly can.

They've done some fire control or something since I was here last. The tangled shrubbery which protected the rockbed from casual drivers has been clipped back, and they've thinned the undergrowth too. I can see again. Running has blown my tears away.

I dive off the main road once I reach the entry point. I've always been proud of the grace with which I can negotiate the small rocks and shrubs leading up to the cliff edge. This morning is no exception.

Tiny rock to tiny rock. Jump over the flannel flowers. Duck under the spiderweb. A welcome, distracting, obstacle course. No twigs snap beneath my shoes. No pebbles cascade down to the road. No trace is left to follow. The gorge plummets below me; a lone gumtree stretches out above. I can hear even more lawnmowers in the distance, tangling with the bird songs. It is Sunday morning after all, AKA Mow-Your-Lawn-if-it's-not-Too-Yellow time.

I reach my rock, sit down, and weep, really weep, for the second time since we found out. I weep for my sister, and the pain that is coming, and the unknown. I weep for my parents. I weep for myself. Then my tears stop. Annoyance sparks. It's only been what? Fifteen minutes? I left church – ingloriously – for these tears. They have no right to dry up so suddenly.

I lie back, resting my head on hard rock littered with brown nuts, and stare up at the sky. Expectant. *God?* In movies, this would be the swelling moment of epiphany when the sun breaks out of the storm clouds. Unfortunately, it's already shining.

An ant bites me. Another plays Follow-the-Leader. 'Ow!' I roll over, scrabbling on the abrasive surface, sweeping away tiny, inquisitive bodies. 'Ow, ow...' A tiny nut embeds itself in the palm of my hand. It is agony, condensed to the size of a thumbtack. '...OW!'

The gorge, overflowing with the tops of trees metres and metres away, does not reply. I glare suspiciously at the rock, until I find a spot to perch that isn't an ant nest. Then I laugh and laugh. It's not hysteria, but hilarious realisation. An hour ago I was getting ready for church, priding myself on my fortitude, especially compared to *some people*. I had believed I was the brave one, stepping out, chin raised – only to promptly run away, unable to cope, unable to explain. Face swollen, eyes throbbing, a complete mess of inadequacies and apprehension.

At least Jasmine knew her weakness, if weakness it is. It apparently takes an ant-ridden rock off the side of the road for me to acknowledge mine. 'Oh God!' I'm burbling, there's no other word for it. 'Forgive me. I'm an idiot. I'm *such* an *idiot*.' I can't stop laughing. Okay, maybe there's *some* hysteria here.

'I can't do this. I need You. I can't be brave.' Then it's gone. All my emotion in one fell swoop, as though it leapt off the cliff edge and fell amongst the trees. I wait for it to return. It doesn't. I'm empty. Finally I stand up, because that's what you do. I wipe my face, because that's what you do as well.

Breaking out of the bush, I feel lighter. A few millilitres of salty water doesn't do that. Seeing God humble you does. The embarrassment of running away still stiffens my shoulders and makes my chin waver upwards, so I walk back to church slowly. This hill has been called 'Heartbreak Hill'. The label's a gross exaggeration, but it gives me time to think.

Could this lesson in humility which God has just taught me be the reason for Jasmine's brain tumour? Could it possibly be 'the good' which he promises to bring out of evil? If so, Jasmine won't die. She won't get any complications. Everything will go back to the way it always was. Except of course, I will be a bit humbler. *Lesson learned, Lord!*

I pull myself up the hill, and in the very furthest recesses of my consciousness, a tendril of hope unfurls.

Surely this nightmare will be over before I know it.

Chapter Five: The Very Last Hour

The garage door slams. 'There you are! I was wondering when you were going to get home. I'm just about to leave.' I run down the stairs to the front door, tying the stays of my karate uniform as I go. 'Was my car in the way? I moved it because I figured you'd want the garage, but—' I break off as Mum and Jasmine spill into the foyer, shedding handbags and shoes and the mail from the letterbox.

Hot. Tired. Hungry. I don't need to be a mind-reader to know that's how they feel. But there's something else as well. Something less common. I can see it scrawled across their faces, tucked into the folds of their mouths like termites in a nest. *Fear?*

How long ago did they leave? The house had been empty when I'd arrived home from uni. The hospital is just over an hour drive away so that meant the appointment took—

'Aren't you going to ask?'

'I need surgery.'

They speak at the same time. I glance from Mum to Jasmine. A few days ago the latter would be in tears. Now her face is simply smeared with that strange expression. It's not Fear. It's Terror.

'When?' I sit on the carpeted stairs.

'In two weeks,' Mum pauses at the top of the other, descending, flight of stairs. 'We have to go in the day before for the pre-op appointment. Then she'll be in the Children's Hospital for two weeks after that, and then she needs hormone treatment—'

'Two weeks!' I latch onto her first piece of news. We've waited so long for information, and now I'm struggling to digest it. I want to give it back, spit it out like a piece of gristle. 'That's... that's so soon.'

'The fifteenth,' Jasmine says. Still quiet. Still sort of... frozen. Her long brown hair is tied in a messy ponytail and her thin arms are wrapped around her school uniform. She looks twelve years old. Too young for a brain tumour.

'They need to do it before she loses her sight altogether.' Mum's steady tone tells me she's already moved beyond these concrete answers and into the realms of conjecture. No wonder she's terse.

I struggle to keep up. 'The fifteenth. That's—'

'The earliest date they can operate.'

'—the day after my 21st birthday.' Stupid me. Stupid selfish me. Stupid tumour-free me. 'Not that it matters!'

'We can do something early...'

Mum meets my eyes as Jasmine moves up the stairs towards her bedroom. 'It doesn't matter.' I repeat. Any attempt to celebrate in the days leading up to the 15th will be a hollow, sad, guilty mockery. I don't want that.

She nods. Even her fringe is sagging in exhaustion. 'I'd better get dinner.' Then she's heading downstairs and I can hear Jasmine upstairs. I'm left behind in limbo, neither up nor down. I slip off my socks and grab my keys. The tiled foyer is cool and not-quite smooth beneath my feet. Perhaps I should stay. Reflect. Digest. Understand. Karate can wait.

No. I've had long enough to ponder. This new information is simply a confirmation of what I already know. What I already fear. If I can't leave the house and enjoy karate like nothing has happened, what will I do tomorrow, and the day after that? What will I do on my birthday?

You're an adult, I say silently, *and a tumour-less one. Stop making a soap opera out of nothing.* I stand alone beside the overflowing shoe-stand. Dad will have a fit when he sees it, yet somehow I suspect it will be the last item raised at the dinner table tonight. *No soap operas,* I promise my black, knee-high gumboots. Then my watch ticks over, and suddenly I'm late.

'*Os!*' Shout the starched white people, and because I'm starched and white, I shout too. The word means 'yes' in Japanese at our karate dojo, so for a frantic moment I try and guess from the stances of the rest of my class what I've just agreed to. *Idiot,* I tell myself, and then undo the chastisement by glancing at the clock high up on the wall. Only half way through.

I wonder if Jasmine has come down to dinner tonight. Dad will know everything by now. These thoughts have been circling each other in my thoughts for the past half hour, like carrion crows hungry for my attention. It's frustrating. Far above most of my class in age – although, tragically, not height – I never, ever, take my karate lessons for granted. Partly because they are expensive. Mostly because I've fought so hard to get where I am.

Literally.

Karate is my love, but certainly not my talent. Next to kids half my age I feel like some sort of benign but slow-witted giant. I try and work doubly hard to make up for my decided lack of spatial awareness. These days when I throw a punch my eyes stay open. I am insanely proud;

it's taken years of training to overcome this unfortunate and decidedly dangerous reflex.

I go through the moves of the *kata,* squatting until my legs ache, pushing aside the air with brutal force. Yet before I can complete the set, the dark crows snatch my thoughts away once more. Two weeks. Then hormone therapy. The future stretches out. It's only been thirty minutes since I heard the news, but crossing the border from reality to speculation has not been difficult.

'Get your sparring gear and a drink. You have thirty seconds!'

'*Os!*' I stick my mouth guard in first to prevent conversation and the taste of stale, salty saliva makes my tongue curl. My gloves I leave dangling around my wrists while I grab my water bottle. The water does nothing to refresh my palate, being old and warm, with the distinct taste of diluted body odour. I care even less than usual.

The little kids tear around on the mats, snatching twenty seconds of freedom before the *sensei* orders them into neat rows. The young teens gossip in a bunch, five boys flexing their legs and smoothing their hair in front of the single girl. A few adults rub sore knees and swap stories of injuries and awful bosses and their children's achievements.

I head onto the floor alone and tuck my sticky fingers into the warm foam of my gloves. I haven't bothered with my shin pads. What are a few bruises today?

Before the MRI Mum had been pressuring me to have a few friends over to celebrate my 21st. I had refused, because I know from experience that it's too much work, and she will end up tired and stressed and then I wouldn't enjoy it. At least there's no party to cancel.

'Get into pairs!'

I jerk. Why can't I stop this selfish mulling? I use my tongue to slip my mouth guard into place and bite down hard on the white plastic. It looks like there's an odd number of ten-year-old boys. The wall clock tells me there's twelve minutes left. Almost there.

'Oi.'

I head over to the boys. They're sorting themselves out in a muddle of gestures and shoves, apparently unaware that one will have to leave the safety of the pack in order to find a sparring partner.

'Oi!' A big south-east Asian man with greying hair moves between me and my target group. A red and white mouth guard dangles from one hand. A belt colour above me, he dismisses the ten-year-olds with a single sweep of his red gloved fist. 'Fight me?'

If I fight the ten-year-olds I can get away with minimum effort and even minimum attention. Particularly if I choose my partners wisely. If I fight this bear of a man he will keep me on my toes. His eyebrow rises in challenge as he slots his mouth guard in.

I smile around my own mouth guard, catch it with my tongue before it can slip out, and acquiesce with a sharp nod and grunt. My response is driven by one of my moral codes, one of my passions, and a good deal of common sense: Never choose the easy path. Nothing trumps the adrenaline of a good fight. This man is older, twice my size, and a senior belt, and I owe him my respect.

We circle slowly. My belt is still new and inflexible, and I am afraid it might not hold its knot. I want to fight well. Not simply because I have just graded to blue belt, but as a thank you…

A combined grading for blue and purple levels. Excited kids, confident kids, laconic kids. All with their proud parents. One adult, a Kiwi, re-grading after moving to Australia. She used to be a black belt; no nervousness in her eyes.

And me.

I am alone. I didn't ask my parents to come. It's an awkward time in the evening and I would be embarrassed to fail in front of them. I scrape through gradings by the skin of my teeth. Pass. Pass. Pass. I don't get distinctions; there's not much to entice an audience.

Yet audience I have. It's the last grading of the night. There should be no uniformed karatekas left, but there is. One huge man, impossible to miss, sitting in the front row near my karate bag. His greying hair is combed over his dark skin and his uniform buckles over his broad shoulders.

I go over in the drink break and fumble for my bottle.

'You okay?'

Gradings leave your muscles shaking, your underclothes soaking wet, your brain numbly circulating Japanese phrases. Right now I could sleep until Google becomes obsolete. 'Yes.'

'You look fierce.' He nods in approval. I can feel my eyes burning, glaring in concentration.

That night I grade with a distinction.

'Hajime!'

I pull my red-padded fists up to my chin but keep my arms loose. We're just out of arm's reach from each other. Often I attack first, but tonight my energy is still sitting in the foyer at home. Probably chatting to the shoe stand. Consoling it after Dad's cleaning spree.

'Ah!' He runs at me, both arms raised. Intimidation, hey? I turn my instinctive flinch into a drop down, deep seated stance. I can never match his height, but I can get down low and secure my centre of gravity.

I throw a punch. He blocks. Twists. Instead of circling mechanically like some of the younger kids do, he comes at me again on the oblique. I side step and bounce on my toes, hands out in front. I grin behind my mouth guard, ferociously alive behind the hair clinging to my neck. Nothing can match the exhilaration of a fight.

He raises an eyebrow. *Come on.*

Today is not the day for strategy. I launch a flurry of punches, then throw out a kick – and hit the ground. *Ow.* Anger rushes in. My kick was slow enough for him to catch. *Idiot.* I push myself off the thin mat and propel myself towards him. Punch.

Deflected. Punch. Head strike. Blocked. I dance back and then forward. If I can only get under his guard - without warning he's under mine, brushing my hands away, peppering me with light punches. I hit everything I can reach and go for a lot more that I can't.

He shoves me away, and pulls out his mouth guard in one movement. I almost don't pause. 'What are you doing?' He shakes his head. 'Concentrate! You're letting yourself get angry and your fighting's sloppy.' His eyes liquefy with disappointment and he opens a target on his side, as if we're training.

I flush and attack him on his protected side instead. This is not about thanking him any more. My motive has become far more primal. I have to win – need to win – *something* tonight.

There are many times I have been grateful a mouth guard prevents proper speech. This is one of them. I shift to the right and close the distance between us. Then, ignoring a fourth target he's opened up, I attack. It is sloppy. I just want to punch something.

He deflects me, and then comes in with a roundhouse kick. *Offph*. I'm on the floor again, but only for a moment. Punch. I can no longer see the other students revolving around us. It's just me and him. Punch. I'm barely penetrating his defences, but his blows are hitting their target each time. They're light with a kindness which only triples my anger.

'Alright, line up!'

We normally fight several rounds. I glance at the clock for the twentieth time and discover the class is finally over. I bow to my partner and turn to flee. His hand stops me. I shake it without meeting his eyes. 'Thanks.'

'Line up!'

I rush to kneel at the front of the dojo. He can't follow because we sit in belt order. Sweat pours down my chin. I tense my arms, hands on my knees, and my elbows tremble.

'*Sensei ne rei!*'

'*Os.*' I bow, never letting my eyes dip from the front of the room. Always watch your opponent, even at rest.

'Sempai ne rei!'

'*Os!*' I bow again, and we're released.

One wipe at my soggy face, and I push my gloves and mouth guard into my bag. Normally I help clear the mats. Not tonight. I find my keys. There's no stopping me now. I look up. He's coming towards me. My only escape route is the main door. He's standing in front of it.

'Emily.' He speaks so gently, so softly. 'Today. Your fighting...'

I don't want to hear it. My sister has a brain tumour, okay? I don't get a 21st like the rest of the population. Why aren't I allowed to lose control, just once?

'Are you okay?'

The dreaded question. 'Yeah, I'm okay.' I grin, because that's what you do. He grins back, but his dratted eyebrows are still raised, and I know I need to offer him something else, something like: My sister has a brain tumour. 'Just tired.'

He nods, and then bows. He's such a big man that it's a whole-body movement. 'Blue belt,' he says, and he's kind enough that all I can detect is respect and congratulations. I deserve irony. 'See you Saturday.'

'Yeah.' I won't be there. Maybe I won't be here ever again. Who can know the future now? 'Thanks for... everything.'

'*Os,*' he says. It's more than a 'yes,' more even, than a mere answer. It's yet another sign of respect I don't deserve.

I only just remember the requisite bow at the door. Ripping off my belt I hurry down the concrete stairs to the underground carpark, the fire exit slamming shut behind me. I pass through the rows of cars and my white uniform is mirrored for a moment on each metallic surface. A hundred glancing ghosts, and she hasn't even died yet. I reach my own car, climb into the driver's seat, undo the stays of my uniform, and burst into tears.

I don't want Jasmine to be sick. I don't want to be strong. I can't be strong. I can't even take my feelings away for one hour without them bubbling over into sloppy fighting and stupid frustrations. I can't even manage to say thank you for kindnesses I don't deserve. It's not fair! My birthday has been ruined and I've spent the past decade processing Mum's illness and now God has given me a fresh tragedy. In my mind's eye, I see Self-Pity, and it's a mauve mist, delicate and tempting. I long to reach out and snatch it to my chest. I long to thrust my nose into its depths and breathe in its cloying scent and *complain*.

I start the engine and navigate through the dark car park and merge onto the narrow street. I'm met with explosions of orange and red and yellow, crowding the night sky. I blink and reach to adjust my glasses before I realise the problem. I wipe my eyes, reducing the riot back into street lamps and brake lights. The clarity lasts through the first roundabout and then everything dissolves into a van Gogh painting once more.

What should I do? I can't stop - but I won't let my parents have two daughters in hospital simply because I was silly enough to drive and cry at the same time.

Squinting, I take a breath and I shout words out one by one. I pound them into being through sheer force. I yank meaning and truth out of the syllables, and no one in their right mind would ever call this singing. Even to myself I sound like a drowning cockatoo.

Yet slowly, the darkness around me softens. The words I sing – old words, new words, words written by other believers in other places – do something to the night. Its downy anonymity becomes comforting, more comforting than I know the gauzy mauve could ever be.

My voice doesn't crack. It's too tear-logged for that. It just disintegrates mid-sentence, crumpling into nothingness, offering me a way back to Self-Pity. But I don't want that anymore, so I swallow the ragged remains of my breath and start again, shouting furious hymns into the darkness until the orbs of light settle to appropriate sizes, and my fists are sore from smashing the steering wheel – and I finally begin to believe the words.

Karate is the simplest form of fighting. A mere exchange of blows. There are no messy opinions or hopeful considerations to trip you up, because you always fight alone. The rules of engagement mean even the kindest friend is your competitor, and the formal dojo rules make it easy to shut them out.

But I can't do that with Jasmine's brain tumour. I can't live one minute of 'this' alone – and the stakes are too high to even attempt it. I've already left my childhood heroes far behind. I failed bravery by fleeing from church, and I flunked stoicism by letting my fury impact my fighting, and my old heroes have nothing else to offer me.

Neither does my old world. My final karate class for the term is over, and with it, my last sixty minutes in a world where I could choose not to speak of Jasmine's brain tumour. There's a date for the surgery now, and the future has been hammered in place. I can't dial back to a pre-tumour era. The old fortress lies behind me, but the drawbridge has been pulled up and there's no way to return.

From here on in, I'll be walking through a landscape where everything familiar has been turned on its head. The speed is picking up and the stakes are rising. A wrong turn could mean death, or something worse. I'm on a quest, a dangerous quest, and no one's told me what we're searching for.

With a shaky breath I reach out in the only direction I am still certain exists in this world where little sisters have brain tumours and surgery dates loom: Heavenward. *Help me!*

Chapter Six: Surgery

'This is ridiculous!' Dad shoves his hand against the steering wheel, surveying the road through his windscreen.

'It's alright, we have plenty of time.' I have to lean forward to speak. I'm sharing the back seat with Jasmine: my nearness is all I can offer. Pretending to look at Dad, I watch her instead.

'Look at that idiot.' A car in front weaves dangerously through the morning peak hour traffic, Dad's shoulders bunch as though he's preparing to physically thrust aside the banked cars, a modern day Moses parting the Red Sea by strength alone.

'They're hardly going to start the operation without her.' I smirk and continue to watch. Did Jasmine's face twitch at my joke, or at something else entirely? I shift sideways in my seat. 'Shall I braid your hair?'

I'm not usually the mothering sort. Courteous eggshell stepping and questions beginning 'shall I' are not normally prominent factors in our sister relationship either. Yet these last few weeks have proved that even breathing too loudly can be volatile. It took sheer bullheaded courage and a secret fear of *what if this is my last chance?* to pray aloud with Jay as we left home in the pre-dawn. Now the featureless morning has given way to honking commuters and a hairstyle is all I have left to give.

'Okay.'

I'm good at braiding and pour all of my desire to *do something, do anything, to fix this* into two tight, even plaits. They hang symmetrically behind each ear, and take all of five minutes. 'Thoughts?' Eggshells or not, I simply have to pierce Jay's pale, tight-with-apprehension exterior. If you can't have significant conversations in the hours before brain surgery, when can you? *Don't you see?* I want to shout. *You don't have to do this alone.*

She twists to see herself in the car rear view mirror. 'Looks good.'

I'm momentarily thrown. I hadn't been asking about her hair.

As we near the hospital, Dad's glances at the car radio clock grow more frequent. 'Dad, just drop me off with her,' I say. 'You can find a park and meet us there.'

'I should be with her.'

'You *will* be with her. As soon as you find a park.' I exaggerate my exasperation. Please think it's confidence. Think it's adultness. I'm twenty-one. Does it really matter if I've only been this age for twenty-four hours?

Jay is even paler now, and her hands are twisting and somersaulting endlessly in her lap. I notice her ears, really notice them, for the first time, because the tight mouse-coloured braids have thrust them into the limelight. Or possibly because today every part of her has become significant, sacred.

They're tiny little things. Pink and soft, and studless today like a newborn baby's. In an hour the surgeon's knife is going to slice open the unmarred skin a few centimetres away, break through her nasal cavity, and burrow up towards her brain. The entire routine is a grotesque mimic of Ancient Egyptian embalming, with one difference. This body will at least start the procedure alive.

'Okay, okay!' Dad turns the wheel sharply. 'Here we are, where will I meet you?'

We're on the kerb outside the hospital. Our review mirror is crowded with stalling taxis and patient transport vehicles. I'm not sure if it's faith in me or necessity which has forced Dad to give in. I suspect the latter and clamp down on the panic billowing behind my throat. To leave the car is to step closer to the surgeon's knife and the marring of her skin and the unknown. To go with her will make me implicit in either her defacement or her salvation – depending on which way you look at it. Can I do it? I have to.

'I don't know, just ring me.'

'Where will I meet you?' Dad repeats.

'Ring me!' I shout, and jump from the car.

Jay insists on carrying her 'personal effects' bag, leaving me with nothing to do but clutch my phone in one hand and concentrate on making sure my heels hit the laminate floor with a confident click. I cannot falter. I don't deserve to. It's not my operation.

Three hundred metres past the double glass doors and I slow down. Which way? Jay doesn't stop. 'Where are you going?' I twist around, half expecting to find battered signs reading: *Jasmine. This Way.* Instead, utterly unhelpful posters inform me of the directions of lifts, toilets and café. 'We have to go to Day Surgery.'

'I know, I came here yesterday, remember? The pre-op?' As I jog to catch up I know she's rolling her eyes. I'm supposed to be the adult here, and I'm beginning to suspect I'm doing a bad job.

In my novels, 'the corridor goes on forever' is an example of hyperbole, but today it is the literal truth.

'Hello?'

'Hi, my name's Emily, and...' *my sister has a brain tumour and she looks far too young and all of a sudden* I *feel far too young...* 'My sister Jasmine Maurits has an operation booked today to remove a pituitary adenoma?'

The nurse lowers her eyebrows, shuffles her paperwork, finds the right forms, gives Jay a smile and slides the papers across the counter. 'We need someone to sign the consent.'

'I'll sign it.'

'And you are...?'

'Her older sister.'

'Age?'

'Twenty-one.' Has anyone ever actually tried to sneak *into* surgery? Does she think we're staging some sort of elaborate hoax?

She hands the pen over. I don't need to bother trying to squash my triumph, it's quickly overtaken by fear. *Are you signing her death warrant?* Shut up, Emily. Stop trying to make yourself feel something. Stop dredging up bad lines of bad movies to make this moment more significant than it is. I lean over Jasmine. 'Do you need help?'

'What do I do for 'patient cover'?'

Absolutely no idea. 'Let me see.' We muddle through the forms. By that, I mean Jay fills them out and I try and divert her attention every time she starts to bite her lip. My success rate is about fifty percent. I'm afraid to touch her. What if I give her a hug and she breaks into pieces before the doctors have a chance to do it properly? At least they know how to put her back together. I hope.

She's weighed, measured, questioned. Have you eaten anything? Are you pregnant? Jay smirks at me. I smirk tentatively back. How different this would all be if her reproducing cells were part of a baby and not a tumour.

A broad-shouldered nurse takes her blood pressure. It's very high. The woman clucks. 'If it continues like that we'll have to call a Code Crimson.'

I read terror in Jay's eyes as she begins to sniffle. The nurse leaves the alcove to pack away the blood-pressure cuff, still muttering to herself, and I storm after her. 'Excuse me. Excuse me!'

She turns.

'You can't say that.' I blurt. 'You've scared her. She doesn't know you're joking. She doesn't know what a Code Crimson is.' *She thinks she's going to die.*

'It's very high.' The nurse gives no ground. 'If it goes outside the parameters—'

'She's scared.' I bite, and don't trust myself to say anything else. I'll cry or scream or both. I march back to the room where a new nurse is giving Jay a white gown.

'Emily, there you are! You've filled out the wrong patient cover! She's a private patient, not a public one...'

Dad comes barrelling in, dragging what I feel like is the least important part of the entire morning into prime position. I guess he's found a parking spot, but I don't want to hear about that either. Jay takes the gown and we escape into the female change room.

The tiled room is empty, a chilling oasis from the production-line we've been on since we entered the hospital. 'Do you need a hand?'

'No.'

Jasmine's in the cubicle for a few too-short minutes, which I spend gathering my tears and herding them back behind my eyelids. When she reappears, she's terrifying. I blame the white gown. Its uninterrupted swathes shrink her even further and in doing so, create something alien. She's an elfin girl with an unmarked face and two light brown braids. Face grey from fear and fasting.

I tie her stays tighter and fix a braid. Neither action is necessary. Jay washes her hands with tiny, delicate splashes. I feel sick. This is how people die. It's in all the books. Angelic girls waste away, like Beth from *Little Women*. 'Too good for this earth' and all that rubbish. I've always hated those perfect girls, found them intensely boring, yet also enjoyed the drama their death brings to the story. Jay has never seemed even remotely angel-like to me, so I always knew she'd live a long and happy life.

'You hungry?' I tear my thoughts back to the prosaic.

She shakes her head. I force a grin and flick her gown. 'You look like someone out of the Bible!' I snigger.

'Abraham, or someone.' I follow her out of the change room. She's going to die. She's going to die. Today she's going to die.

If only I could rip that stupid white gown off. Why don't they make them in blue or green or yellow poke-a-dots? Why stupid, ethereal *white? Oh God, she's actually going to die, isn't she?* For the first time in my life (so many firsts this morning) I realise that perhaps I don't, no, I *can't*, dislike those girls who look like angels and die young. I can't dislike them, because they can't exist. So I close my eyes and pray for a boring and unpoetic universe. I pray for a world where no one's angelic, and everybody lives.

'Who's going in with her?' The nurse looks from Dad to me.

'I am,' Dad stands with the air of one prepared to protect his youngest daughter against the world, come what may.

I stand up as well. I have to. 'Who do you want, Jay?'

'Dad.' She looks properly afraid now, her earlier air of self-sufficiency gone. I don't blame her. In the same way I understand her choice, but don't like it. She's going to die. She's going to *bloody* die – I squish her so tightly I can feel her ribs through my breasts. I kiss her too. The time for sisterly off-handedness has passed. 'See you, Jay. I love you very much. It's going to be fine. Remember, God's got a plan.'

My words are too small.

'Ring Mum,' Dad tells me urgently. 'Tell her we're going in.'

I nod. *Let her live. Let her live.* I pace outside the theatre doors. *Nothing good can come out of her death that can't come out of her life.* Who am I trying to convince? I'm not sure, but I know there's only one person who can act. *Oh God, let her live!*

'How'd it go?'

Dad closes the door to the theatre suite like it's a fridge. It clunks and slurps, sealing Jasmine inside. He looks unexpectedly haggard. It's only been ten minutes, but all the wrinkles in his face are in disarray, as though in that time he's been picked up and shaken vigorously.

'She was scared.' I don't recognise his voice. 'It was awful. She fought and fought the anaesthetist.' He brushes the disposable hair net from his head and stares at it in annoyance. 'She kept pulling the mask from her face.' He flattens his grey hair with his other hand. 'She was waving her arms so much I thought she'd take out a doctor! *No, no, no!* she was screaming.'

My stomach shivers. You don't believe in omens, I remind myself.

Then again, there was a lot I didn't believe in before Jay's diagnosis. Dad straightens. 'Come on, let's go to McDonald's.'

They haven't rung. I've drunk a chocolate thickshake and Mum has arrived with Aunty Berna. Coogee McDonald's is bustling with late-morning patrons, and still the hospital hasn't rung.

'Why haven't they rung? It's been three hours. They said in three hours.' Dad says.

'They'll ring soon.'

'Maybe something went wrong,' Dad worries. 'Maybe the tumour was bigger than they thought.'

'Will you stop it?' Mum glares at him.

'You're not helping.' I agree and turn back to my laptop. I've been sifting through fictions woven before I ever had to string the words 'tumour' and 'sister' into a single sentence. Somehow the carefully constructed trials of my beloved characters seem colourless today, robbed of any sense of sacrifice or urgency. Even so, they feel much more real than what's taking place at the Children's Hospital. They have, after all, been part of my life for far longer.

'I'm going to move the car.' Dad stands up. There's still an hour left before the parking limit runs out, but I keep my mouth closed and my eyes on my computer screen. Unlike me, Dad doesn't have a story world to retreat to. Mum and Aunty Berna talk quietly, today's newspaper spread out on the speckled laminate next to their cardboard coffee cups. The crossword is half completed.

Dad gone, I find myself wishing that I too had a car to move. I lean back against the plastic booth instead and breathe in and out. The air tastes like sweaty chips. Jasmine cannot die while I'm sitting in Mcdonald's. She can't. It's not in *any* of the books.

'You should eat something.'

'I will.' I get up, more to get away than because I want to make myself a watery coffee. Why are the waiting rooms outside the operating theatres so tiny?

Aunty Berna frowns and pulls out her plastic wrapped lunch. Mum is testing her blood sugar levels with a pin-prick test. Dad has decided to move Mum's car now.

I can't eat. How can I eat while my sister's brain is being cut open? How can I eat while all the other families in the waiting room have received their good news and left? How can I eat when it's been seven hours and we're sitting here waiting to hear the outcome of a three hour procedure? The chocolate thickshake lurches in my stomach as I pour static instant coffee grains into a styrofoam cup. I add hot water and milk and carry it the three steps back to our row of plastic chairs. It goes cold.

Finally I close my laptop, leaving my heroic characters stuck in an Afghan blizzard. I can't bring myself to care. Instead I pull out my phone and start scrolling. I would know if Jasmine dies, right? Again, it's in all the books. When a loved one dies you're supposed to feel your soul ripping, or something. I mentally prod my chest. I *think* it's still intact.

This is ridiculous. 'I'm going outside.' I leave the tiny room and its silent population. Up down, up down the corridor. Seven steps one way, swivel. Eight steps back. The math doesn't make any sense. Nothing does. Do I have a sign above my head? *'My sister is having a brain operation and we've been waiting seven hours.'* Surely I must. Something this momentous can't possibly remain private.

Why does every passer-by look so disinterested? So busy? Don't they care? I thrust my hands in my pockets to keep myself from temptation. I want to grab one of these calm people and shake them. *Don't you see? This minute right now is important. It doesn't get more important than this!*

Are they blind to Catastrophe crouching at the door? Can't they feel her cool breath against their neck? Jay's death would justify this awful fear. If she dies they would have to notice, *have* to care. Surely not even a hospital corridor can remain efficient and calm if Death strides down it.

Is this how you are going to answer my prayer, Lord? By culling her life before it's even reached its prime? Will she turn into some sort of Sunday school lesson, or a tragic newspaper column? I should have imposed some boundaries all those years ago. 'Save her, whatever it takes, except a brain tumour'. That would have been a better prayer.

Surely even The Worst could not be as bad as this infernal waiting. Surely – A man in blue scrubs enters the tiny waiting room. It's a stimulus which shatters my mechanical stride. I dive in after him.

'Hello? Are you Jasmine's parents?' Then he cocks his head at me and Aunty Berna. 'Jasmine's family?' We're the only people in the room.

'Yes, is she okay?'

'How did it go?'

'Why was it so long? You said—'

He holds up his hand and performs the action we've all been waiting for. He smiles. 'Yes, yes.' He adds several nods to his smile and we relax further. Except for Aunty Berna we're all on our feet in a perfect semi-circle around him. It's as if we have been practising our whole lives for this moment.

'It was an involved operation, as you are no doubt aware, but it was successful. The tumour was a different consistency from what we expected but we think we were able to remove it in its entirety. There was a leak of CSF, that is, spinal fluid, so we patched it up with fat from her stomach, and it should settle down over the next few days. She's waking up nicely in ICU at the moment.'

'Thank you. Seven hours! You must be tired!'

'Can we see her?'

Mum and Dad speak together. I say nothing.

'This way,' he says. 'But only two at a time.'

They leave.

'What a relief,' says Aunty Berna. Again, I say nothing.

I'm impatient long before the double doors spit Dad out with a territorial slurp. I push my way through while they're still trembling, and then stop. Sudden fear ices my throat. What will she look like? Will she still be Jasmine? I know the questions are irrational, but I'm still afraid. I swallow and step forward.

'Excuse me?' The first person I see is a nurse in navy scrubs. 'Where's Jasmine Maurits? I'm her sister.'

'Jasmine? Over to the right.'

There she is. Drowning in white. White gown, white bed, white face half wrapped in bandages – joy eclipses fear and I surge forward. 'Jay!'

'Naaargghhh!' The noise is animal, inhuman.

'Shh!' Mum hisses in something a few decibels lower than a whisper. 'She's got a splitting headache.'

I lean over the bed.

'Naarghh!'

'Don't shake the rails,' Mum says. 'She's very sensitive.'

I bend carefully. 'Oh Jas...' The sheets near her head are splattered with patches of dilute red. Something is leaking. Or was leaking. It's hard to tell with her nose all taped up and tubes spraying out of her nostrils, her hair still covered in a disposable white cap. 'How do you feel?' I breathe.

'IIII feeeelll *craaaap*.' The words are drawn out as though an alien is trying to adjust to human speech patterns and using a very, very drunk individual for their analysis. I flinch. I've never heard her say 'crap' before. I fight a smile.

'It's over, Jay,' I say softly. 'It went really well. It's all—'

'Shhhh...' This time it's Jasmine, not Mum, and it comes out in the same drugged slur. 'My head hurrrrtttss.' Tears trickle down her half-wrapped face and before my eyes she slips mercifully into morphine dreams.

I shove my way through the swinging doors, back into a different world with a tiny waiting room and its single occupant.

'Your dad's gone to move the car,' Aunty Berna says, getting to her feet. 'How is she?'

I sink down and start to cry. Tears of happiness. Tears of relief. Tears of tensions relieved and nightmares excised. Tears I didn't know I had. Tears I can't stop. *It's over.* Aunty Berna wraps me in a hug. It is over, and now it's time for healing. Time for the good things God has promised.

Time to live again.

REFLECTION
Reach out your hands

After Jasmine's first operation I had no idea how many other operations she would have. I didn't realise that the day would come where I would see the Neurology Ward at the Children's Hospital as a sort of home, and home itself as more like a hotel room: a place to sleep and gather together remnants of energy in order to face the next day.

I'm glad I didn't know, but even if I had, I'm not sure it would have made much difference. While operations and waiting never gets easier, they certainly become more familiar. In one sense the first operation is always the hardest, simply because it's first. The first time you have to navigate medical terminology and consent forms; the first time you're faced with the possibility of death-by-surgical-knife; the first time you have to give this particular loved one into the hands of God.

This, I think, is why the weeks surrounding Jasmine's diagnosis were some of the hardest I faced. They were certainly the loneliest. A diagnosis of any kind requires a period of grieving. It's a letting go of life and perhaps even personhood as you understood it, and learning a new identity. It's about figuring out how to live in a universe where things like health or freedom are no longer the constants you thought they were, and grappling with a dawning understanding of what really matters.

And yet, there's always a gap between the time you receive the news of a diagnosis and the time when your circle of friends and family, your particular community, understands what that news looks like. This gap, this abyss, is a lonely and frightening place. Sometimes, for less visible or less comprehensible illnesses, it can stretch for decades.

Ill health and the inside of hospitals were not new for me. My mum has struggled with chronic health difficulties for as long as I can remember. Yet we all have some parts of our lives that we see as incorruptible, untouchable. For me, this was Jasmine. Come sun or rain, come death or tragedy, I always believed she would be safe. When her diagnosis entered our lives, it felt acutely unnatural, almost profane, as though a sacred part of life had been desecrated. In a way it had.

So there it was: the innate fear we all have of the unknown, the grief over an altered universe, the loneliness which comes after communication but before understanding, and the corruption of something - someone — I had believed unassailable. These were the burdens we carried those first weeks. Mingled as they were with the multitude of lesser worries and annoyances we all carry about daily, they formed a crippling load.

If I could somehow stretch through the ether of history and give my past self just one word of encouragement during that time, it would be this: reach out your hands, Emily. People are kinder than you think.

When trouble comes it is easy to retreat. Easy to curl in on yourself and your tragedy. It's hard to trust that others will say the right words or give the right response. It seems impossible to believe that the people flung across your life story will care enough, help enough, *be* enough for you during this time.

The reality is, they won't be enough. We will never receive *enough* in one fell swoop, save from the hand of God. But the people around you are a start, a beginning, a God-given genesis. When we open our hearts to them, we begin to collect bits and pieces of grace. Words, hugs, tears, silences. One by one we collect them, until one day they begin to rival our load of terrors and griefs and lonelinesses. Until one day, we look around and discover we have *enough*.

It's far easier, in the beginning, to retreat and lick your wounds. Yet if we never begin to share fears, accept condolences, or explain anxieties, we will not last the journey. It can take a lifetime to collect *enough* to live gracefully with tragedy. Some people never get there. They die, trusting God, but viewing all of humanity with cynicism and suspicion. And I can't help but wonder, is that really trusting? Can one claim to trust their King, yet refuse to trust their brother?

When I share my turmoil with a friend, is it really them I'm trusting? Or is God, who can use all people and heal all wounds?

In times of hardship, *reach out your hands.* People are kinder than you believe, and God is greater than you think.

PART TWO

Chapter Seven: Miracles, Ordinary and Extraordinary

'**H**ello, Emily speaking.'

'It's Aunty Berna.'

I fumble for an explanation, holding the landline to my ear. Since the operation Jay has been weaving in and out of pain-filled consciousness, her ICU bed wet with tears and sweat. Mum's not well, and I was ordered to 'take a break', so Aunty Berna went to sit by her today. 'How's Jay?'

'The doctors just came around. They're fasting her again, did you know?'

'No! Fasting? Why? Is her spinal fluid—'

'Still leaking. They're going to operate again this afternoon.'

Again? Is spinal fluid dripping from her nose a good enough reason to wheel her back into the theatre? It was only two days ago they wheeled her out! Is this what a 'successful' surgery looks like? Across the kitchen table Mum looks pale and drawn. She's heard enough to understand. I set down the phone.

'How can it be leaking?' she asks.

'I don't know.'

It's a hollow, surreal morning. I plug away at one of my last uni assignments, and note that I should start looking for a post-graduate job. The idea seems ridiculous. By the time Mum is well enough to sit in the car, I'm more than ready to drive.

Parking is a nightmare, as it was yesterday. At least the commute is only for two more weeks… or will this second operation delay her discharge? Please, Lord, take the leak away. *Make it stop.*

'Hey Jay.' My several-decibels-below-a-whisper voice is improving. Practice makes perfect after all, and I've had a lot of practice. The real problem is not *my* voice but Jasmine's. The pain means she can't talk very loudly, so it's difficult to hear her unless I lean on the bed rails, which is still a big no-no.

They are very cautious with doling out pain medication at the Children's Hospital. Good for future addicts; bad for present sufferers. I lean over and sort of drape myself over the air above her. It's the only type of hug you can give to someone who can't move and flinches at touch and noise.

A half smile flickers over the part of her mouth I can see and her eyes brighten for a second. It's nice, and the realisation that it's nice drags me back a decade…

'Just play dolls with her for an hour, Emily. That's all.' Mum is using her I'm-at-the-end-of-my-tether voice.

'But Mummm…' I push a tissue into my library book to mark my progress. The five children have almost caught the chimpanzee villain. 'It's boring.'

'Well, you can make it not boring. She's your sister. You always wanted a little sister.'

I roll my eyes. Maybe when I was five years old. Maybe before I realised little sisters like to play Barbies and host imaginary tea parties. 'I hate dolls.'

'Maybe she'll want to play stuffed animals with you?'

Maybe she will. But I won't, because I don't play stuffed animals. I use them to tell stories. Stories Jay wouldn't like. I try to imagine Jay 'helping' to guide my horse and dog through an elaborate plan to escape from the cruel farmer. She'll want to rescue them too early. She won't let the dog die to save the other animals, and she'll start crying when the unicorn arrives too late to heal his wounds. It would be a disaster. 'Alright. I'll play dolls.'

'Remember, she wants to spend time with you because she loves you.'

Sure.

Is one operation, and the threat of another, really enough to bridge the four year gap between us? To fix us? Surely this is simply a blip in the radar, a reflex action because she almost died. Whatever it is, I like it, and I'm going to enjoy it. In hospital Jay's not too old for hugs, and I've got a lot I never gave. It's almost like a second chance.

'We brought some cards,' I say. 'You've got at least four times more than I have, so I can't imagine what *your* 21st birthday will be like. Mostly people at church, but some school friends messaged your phone. Wanna see?'

Her head nod is minuscule, a quiver of bandages. I pull out a card. Pink butterflies and bright flowers.

'Can you see it?' Mum asks.

A microscopic shake. Mum's forehead creases. The doctors have told us it will take a while for Jasmine's central vision to clear after the operation because the tumour was pressing on her optic nerve. It's too early to judge whether there's been permanent damage, but that doesn't mean we don't try.

'How about these big words?' Mum's voice verges on desperate. 'Can you see those? They say 'Get Well Soon!''

'Oww, Muum.'

'Sorry,' Mum winces. She flips open the card and brings her voice down. 'I'll read the inside message.'

It's probably a really nice message, full of verbal hugs and optimism, but I'm not listening. I watch as Jay slowly reaches out a hand between the bed bars. Her fingers are wrapped in gauze to protect the cannula, leaving her with a stump. The stump brushes stiffly against the printed flowers. It's a sad, mute gesture, and I swallow as Mum puts the card down. 'Guess what, Jay?' I blurt, 'I have a funny story. You wouldn't believe what happened the other day...'

Her eyelids sag in response and I hear a snore.

'Are my story-telling skills that bad?' I mix mock indignation and genuine astonishment into what feels like the perfect cocktail. 'She didn't even let me get to the punch line!' Mum stretches her tired face into a smile. We gaze at what little we can see of Jasmine beneath the sheets and the bandages and the tubes.

'You were right,' I say, eyeing the bulging catheter bag hanging off the bed. 'About the diabetes insipidus.' Mum nods. I can tell she's travelling in the future again.

They told us yesterday that Jasmine's water balance is permanently 'out'. She's going to be on medication to manage it her entire life. The booklet the hospital provided is grim. It delivers warnings in comic sans font about always being near a water source and the dangers of dehydration. Apparently balancing your body's need for water artificially is 'not easy'. Mum, more than anyone, knows what health professionals mean when they use those words.

Wasn't a brain tumour enough? Surely when they talk of medical alert bands and say 'permanent' they don't *really* mean *for the term of her natural life*? Surely once she's out of hospital everything will be alright?

'Thirssssty.' Just as quickly as she fell asleep, Jay wakes.

'You're only allowed ice,' Mum says, 'because of the operation.' She holds the styrofoam cup to Jay's lips.

Jasmine gives a soft groan. Water seeps into her pillow. It's hard to suck ice when you're lying horizontal. 'Want water,' she mutters.

I glance at the swollen drip bag dangling above her shoulder. She won't dehydrate. Still, when her fluids are in such delicate balance anyway... 'Wanna play I Spy?' I ask. Best not to think about it too much. Best pretend I'm the trusting type.

Jasmine peers at me out of one eye, the other mashed against her bedsheets. Her lips flicker. 'Okay.'

'You go first.' Please, convince me you're still my sixteen-year-old sister, rather than this half mute, incredibly sensitive person in a hospital bed.

'Nooo.'

The morale of the hospital room teeters dangerously. Mum's reading yet another pamphlet, frowning. A bag of laughs these information sheets are. Where did she get that one? Time to turn things up a notch. Big smile. 'Alright, I spy with my little eye something that starts with… B.'

'Hospital?'

'That starts with H.' I can't look at Mum. The surgeon said there was no brain damage, he said… I squeeze my lips together and pull the handbrake on my terrified thoughts.

'Oooh. I forgooot.' Jay twitches.

I wait. And wait. Has she forgotten the game as well?

'Bed?'

I breathe out. 'Nope! It's really easy.' Bigger smile. Brighter voice.

'Ummmm…' This is going to be a slow match.

'Blanket?'

'Yes! Your turn.' I twist around in my chair while I wait for her to choose something, trying to figure out what is actually in her line of view. The disposable blue curtain; the yellow and red assist buzzers; the nurses' station, their counter piled high with patient folders; Mum testing her blood sugars and looking even more tired than before; a spare blue visitor chair and — I turn back. Her eye is closed.

She's fallen asleep again.

'Hello! You must be Jasmine's mum and...'

'Sister.' I smile up at the nurse. She's small and lively looking in her navy scrubs, long blonde hair tied back into a ponytail, upside-down watch pinned on her chest.

'Oh nice,' she smiles back. 'Younger?'

I stare. 'Older.' and then as if I need to convince her, 'I'm in my last year of uni.'

'Oh,' she smiles on, 'What're you studying?'

'Radiography.'

'Ooh, you should get a job here!' She tosses her head. 'How is Jasmine going?'

'Sleeping.' Mum says.

I roll my eyes. 'Again.'

'Any news about when the surgery is?' Mum focuses on the thing I've been trying to ignore.

'That's why I'm here.' The nurse shuffles some papers. 'Besides to do her obs. of course. We've just got the doctor to review the amount of spinal fluid coming from her nose, and he's spoken to the Neuro Team. They think we can stop fasting her for now; it's not enough to warrant another operation.'

'Really?'

'You mean it will heal on its own?' Mum. Ever the practical one. I'm still in mild shock.

'Hopefully. She'll be reviewed tomorrow morning of course, but for now she can eat.'

Thank you, God! Thank you. The nurse performs the obs. and empties Jasmine's catheter bag. She measures the molten gold and adds the number to an already lengthy chart. When the Water In/Water Out table stops tallying, it's time for the next dose of Jasmine's medication. Too little of the medication and Jasmine's catheter bag needs to be changed every thirty minutes; too much and her body will start to swell from all the fluid she's retaining, leading to heart failure. 'Remember,' the nurse continues, 'You can eat and drink to thirst, but you still need to write it all down so we can give you the right dose of anti-diuretic.'

'Yeees,' Jasmine is awake and blinking.

'Yes,' Mum and I echo. As the nurse leaves I pick up a typed paper slip and pen from the rolling bedside table: today's food choices. 'What do you want, Jay?' I ask with all the grandeur of a waiter introducing a seasonal menu at a posh restaurant.

'Nothing.' She begins to cry.

'What's wrong? Are you in pain?' Mum moves as close to the bed rails as she can get. 'I'll call the nurse.'

'Not hungry,' Jasmine slurs. 'I feel sick.'

'You haven't eaten for...' I try and calculate. 'At least a day and a half. Are you sure you're not hungry?'

'Maybe your stomach feels sick because it's empty.'

Jasmine frowns at Mum's suggestion. 'Noo.' Then she stops and blinks. 'My stomach just vibrated.'

'*It what?*' Mum and I stare.

'Something's vibrating!' Tears gather at the corners of her eyes. Her lips shake.

'Do you want me to feel it?' Mum asks. 'Whereabouts?'

'No touch...' Jasmine's nostrils flare.

Mum looks as helpless as I feel. Vibrations weren't on the list of side-effects. Then it comes to me. 'Jay, is your stomach grumbling?'

It's *her* turn to stare. She thinks hard, with all the obviousness of a two-year old. Or a sick sixteen-year-old. Then her mouth twitches. 'Yes!' she says, face lighting up like she's discovered it's Christmas. *'That's it!'*

We burst into appropriately quiet laughter.

Mum and I stop at the shops on our way home. Jasmine's slowing leak has given us energy. Surely it will be cleared up by tomorrow. Surely no more operations are needed.

'I'll ring you when I'm done,' I say as we step out of the car. The carpark is dark and crowded. Mum's getting necessities; I'm picking up my free birthday Subway. It's been three days since I turned twenty-one and it feels like a decade. Not that it matters. Nothing matters now except that Jasmine's leak is closing up. She'll be home soon!

'No carrot or jalapenos. Thanks.' I walk back to the main shops slowly, clutching my warm bread roll and enjoying the solitude. Mum doesn't answer the first two calls on her phone so I text instead. It's 5 pm and the centre is full of people 'dropping in' after work. Or at least that's what I assume. They could just as well be returning from a hospital, like us.

That's the thing with crowds. You never know where the individuals inside them have come from or where they are going. People complain about hospitals having a distinct smell, but even if that's true it is not one strong enough to follow you home or mark you in a crowd. Whether that's a relief, I'm not sure. My sandwich is cooling rapidly. I use my free hand to ring twice more but reach Mum's voicemail each time. *Where is she?*

I send three texts. No reply. Did she even make it into the shops? It's so dark and busy out there. She can't see well as it is. What if she got hit by a reversing car? Don't be silly. Is this what visiting a hospital does to you? Convince you that death and accident are lurking in every corner? Pull yourself together, she's fine.

I jiggle for a second. Would Mum go back to the car? There'd be little point: I have the keys. She was so dizzy and unwell this morning. Perhaps something *has* happened. I'd better check inside the shop. I enter, twitching at the assistant's 'hello'. Instead of seeing the shelves of food and clothes and cosmetics, I see the dark car park, the red reverse lights, and myself speaking to a paramedic...

'You can't bring her to hospital,' I beg, looking down at the crumpled figure on the bitumen. 'My sister's already in the Children's with a brain tumour. Please, I can't have two family members in hospital!'

I see surprise and pity on his face, both of which make my blood simmer—

Stop! I shake my head and slow my jog to a brisk walk, weaving around the ridiculously slow shoppers. Where on earth is Mum? She's not here. I've checked the entire store. She can't *really* be outside in the carpark, can she? I'm tired of feeling scared. I've sent seven text messages and called more times than I can remember. Even if she has her phone on silent, she would have checked it by now. She can't possibly be taking this long. Perhaps she's back at the car after all. I head towards the front of the shop.

'Is Emily there? Emily? Your Mum's here. Please come to the front desk.'

I jerk. Relief flash floods my system. She's not on the ground of the car park! *She's alive*. I head to the desk and don't even feel embarrassed about the overhead call. 'Mum!'

'Emily! There you are!' Mum grins in relief. She turns to the lady behind the desk. 'That's her! Thank you.'

'Why didn't you answer your phone?' The annoyance I assumed would be on Mum's face surfaces in my own voice. 'I rang a million times!'

'I've lost it! It's not in my bag; I hope I left it in the car.'

I plop my own phone in my handbag with my cold sandwich as we leave the shop and step out into the night. I grip Mum's arm. 'I thought you'd been hit by a car.' It's an admission I might not have made three days ago.

'I thought you'd been abducted!' Mum says in reply, clutching my hand to her side. 'I was thinking, I've almost lost one daughter and now I've lost my second one!'

Oh *fiddlesticks*. This confession is far more shocking than my own. Mum is frustratingly realistic and not at all prone to dramatics. At least, not normally. Then again, having a daughter in hospital with a tumour isn't normal.

We laugh in relief and find her phone down the side of the car. We turn the lights on in our empty house. We jump for the home phone as it rings.

'Hi, it's me.'

'Dad?' Jasmine has eaten some toast, he reports. Her 'vibrations' have stopped and she is feeling much better. There have been no more spinal fluid drips from her nose. Tonight we are all alive. Tonight four people have survived another day.

Tonight I recognise this as the miracle it always is.

The tunnel has a light

DIARY EXCERPT
September 18, 2015 (4 days in hospital)

I've said Job's prayer when things have been terrible, but now I get to say it while things are going well. And that is lovely, and life-inducing. I've learnt not to fall into optimistic hope too easily, because life is hard. Because of that, sometimes happiness or even contentment arrive and surprise me. Not that the tunnel won't be long, and won't be suffocating. Because it will. But there is a light at the end.

The Lord takes away. But He also gives.

"The Lord gave and the Lord has taken away;
may the name of he Lord be praised."
Job 1:21 (NIV)

Although I can be happy when he takes away, it's so *nice* when he gives.

Chapter Eight: The Conversations We Avoid

The queue for McDonald's is so long it has swallowed our small table and is threatening to consume the entire plaza. We can't even move away because the table is bolted to the floor. Are shopping centre managers really afraid someone will run off with a metre square of sticky, pock-marked plastic?

Mum's testing her blood sugar levels. Dad's biting into his burger. Anyone in this crowded underground centre would feel safe to assume we're a happy family of three, having dinner out. They couldn't be more wrong.

'Can I have sushi?'

'Yes,' Mum's tone is so lacking in inflection I'm not sure she's even heard. Maybe, like the rest of us, all her energy is focused on listening for something else. It's well past the proposed completion time of Jasmine's second surgery. Is that a bad thing? Last time it wasn't. Surely they would ring us immediately if something went wrong.

Surgery plans have been made and unmade over the past few days as the doctors try to decide whether or not the pathway from Jay's brain to her nose will close up on its own. It was almost a relief when they told us they were going to operate a second time. I like decisive action, and if Jay's nose can't make up its mind, I'm glad her surgery team can. Then again, it's not my body being cut open...

Beep-bip-beepity-beep! We freeze. We straighten. We dive for the phone. Dad reaches it first, which is unsurprising since it's his phone and sitting in his breast pocket. 'Hello, Paul speaking. Doctor, hello.'

'Loudspeaker!' I hiss. We all lean in. The noise in the shopping centre eats the words as quickly as the phone spits them out. I catch the key ones.

'Went well... as expected... Patched up the leak, lumbar drain placed to redirect spinal fluid. Should dry up... Looks really good... In Recovery.'

Purgatory has ended. I slump back in my seat. 'I'll buy my dinner and then—'

'Just let me collect my—'

'She's okay, she's okay!'

We pick up our lives and head to the nearby hospital, leaving the bustling crowd to tussle like a squabble of seagulls over our vacated table.

The 'good drugs' haven't entirely worn off, but they've relocated Jasmine back to the ward anyway. I suspect Recovery is closing up for the night. She's back in her old bed and more asleep than awake.

'Thirsty,' she mumbles again. Dad holds the lemonade ice-block to her lips. For a moment they glisten with melting sugar, and then she pushes it away with a wrinkled nose. 'I've been thinking,' she announces.

I lean forward. I'm tired — we've been here since early morning — but I don't want to miss a word. My stomach still hurts from laughing in Recovery. This time around Jasmine was far more chipper coming out of the anaesthetic haze. She kept calling the surgeon 'Doctor Noodle' and it had been difficult to get her to stop talking long enough to answer the nurses' questions. 'Yes?' Mum asks. 'What've you been thinking?'

'About our church.'

Our church? I'd been expecting a pronouncement on the philosophy of ice-blocks or a new pet-name for Dad.

'Yes.' She speaks as if every word is an effort. I can tell she's teetering on the edge of consciousness. 'Our church is very supportive, aren't they, Mum? Like that Bible verse. 'All things work for the good of...' she trails off, and frowns, '...of *something*. I've forgotten what.' She doesn't let that stop her. 'But getting a brain tumour helped me see how supportive the church is.' She gives the lip twitch which is her usual post-surgery smile. 'I've been thinking,' she repeats. *'That's* the good.' A second blissful lip twitch, and she closes her eyes.

I stare. Do drugs give you words or, like alcohol, simply reveal what's already there? It's hard to believe that this is Jasmine... clown of the class, life of the party, but nevertheless thinking about things like faith and providence, and after two brain surgeries. *Jesus? Thank you.*

Even as I pray, I'm struck with guilt. Jasmine might have found her 'good', but as I watch her wear bandages like they're this season's latest fashion, too feeble to even smile properly, it simply doesn't seem like *enough*.

A brain tumour, two operations and life-long complications, all for a realisation that God's people *care?* The equation doesn't balance for me.

Then again, I've never been brilliant at maths.

I come late and sit alone. Dad's at the hospital this evening; Mum's resting. The sermon washes over my scattered thoughts like waves over a rock. I give up trying to concentrate after the first Bible reading. I simply don't have it in me. Not tonight.

The songs are another matter. They speak of life and death, hope and glory, realities which I rub shoulders with each time I step into the Neurology Ward. The lyrics on the overhead screen drip with lifeblood so warm it may as well have come from me. I ache as if it has, and my mind drifts to the boy in the bed across from Jasmine. I don't think he'll ever walk again. It's touch and go whether he'll ever be able to tell his parents he loves them.

'Oh how I do wish that the last day was here...
Where sorrow is over, the world is set free,
and that which we hope for we finally see.'

I resurface as the minister stands to say a final blessing. The worship songs and familiar scenes have worked their tonic. I feel sharply refreshed and utterly exhausted, as though I've taken an icy dip after pulling an all-nighter. The old couple beside me turn in their seats. At the beginning of the church service they had gestured me over: 'We can't bear to see you sit alone.' Would they have said that if Jasmine wasn't in hospital? I hate that I question this, but I hate being a pity case too.

Now they ask after Jasmine, and I scramble for both my social skills and Jesus' love. Sometimes being part of God's family is about receiving as well as giving. Besides, I can't deny it's *nice* to be wanted. To feel loved.

A body embraces me from behind. It's one of the older ladies. Out of the corner of my eye I can see several other members of the congregation hovering: Waiting to talk, to ask, not wanting to flood me. 'How is she? How are you?'

I try to answer their questions helpfully. I attempt to convey seriousness hopefully and thankfulness sincerely. Without the hospital backdrop and Jasmine's shaking body centre stage, it feels uncomfortably like I'm reciting someone else's story.

'How are you?' A thin old lady with deep, concerned eyes limps over.

'I'm good. Just tired.'

'So you're better? What a blessing!'

What? I backtrack frantically. Does she… perhaps… Nope. I have no idea. 'Er… What's better?' I ask.

She peers at me. 'Your tumour. It was in your head, wasn't it?'

'Ah… No. That's Jasmine. My sister?'

'Oh yes of course! Silly me. How is she?'

'She's still in hospital. We're praying this second operation will heal the leak completely.'

She nods, looking equal parts embarrassed and distracted. 'Sorry, I knew it was her. I just get a bit forgetful sometimes.'

I smile. I love her. She is gentle and kind. 'I know. It's fine.'

'Well!' She pats me on the arm. 'Don't let me keep you! You should speak to your friends.'

Every time we talk she says this, and every time I wonder when she'll realise I consider *her* my friend. Still, tonight especially, I guess it would be good to talk to people my own age. I glance around but there doesn't seem to be anyone else waiting to ask me questions. I eye the younger group at the back of the church. I know they'll welcome me with open arms and thoughtfulness. I also know they'll give me a chance to talk about something other than hospitals and sick sisters.

I pick my handbag off the carpet and sling it over my shoulder. I don't think I *can* talk about anything else tonight. I don't *know* much about anything else. Jasmine, brain tumours and hospitals are my current subjects and I'm well-schooled in them. It's a very focussed degree. I hope I'll graduate soon.

With quick steps which scream 'I have somewhere to be, don't intercept me,' I cross to the back of the church and out into the emptiness of the foyer. No more conversations. Not tonight.

'I don't want to.'

'You should try.'

'No! Emily...' A whine. 'I don't want to see her.'

'It might be helpful.' I wave my hands. 'To... you know. Talk about things.'

'I don't want to talk to her!'

'You haven't even met her!'

'I have too!' Jay glares at me. 'The chaplain came last week when Mum was here and it was awful.' She twists the corner of the coverlet in both hands. 'Don't make me.'

'It doesn't have to be for long!' Honestly, how difficult could it be to hold a conversation with someone besides Mum and I? But that's the point. She isn't talking to Mum or me. Not really talking. Not this-is-how-I-feel talking. Not since the night of her second operation. I take a breath. How far can I push this? I'm not her parent. The only authority I have over her is what she'll give me. And at home that was nothing. Here? I'm not sure yet...

I test the waters. 'Please, Jay. It would be rude to refuse to see her.'

'You can tell her—'

'I'm not telling her anything.' I fold my arms.

'Oh! You...' Will she scream? Tell me she hates me? It wouldn't be the first time, but I suspect it will hurt more now. Or will she burst into tears so the nurses will come and find out what's wrong? That could be awkward to explain. 'Will you stay with me?'

What? She's asking... she thinks... The way she's looking at me. As if my presence can be a comfort. As if I can protect her against the world. I can't. Not really. But I can certainly try.

'Of course.' I relax my arms, even as my throat thickens. 'I'm not going anywhere. If you think I'm going to spend the morning standing outside in the corridor...'

She scowls at my attempt at humour. It seems she wants me but she hasn't forgiven me. Odd.

'There she is.' Jay whispers.

I crane my neck to see out the window into the hall. Is that the chaplain? I turn to whisper back, and catch myself. I'm the adult here. There's no need to peer around corners like we're in *Spy Kids*. 'Good.' I reply in a consciously normal tone.

Jay pouts. 'Maybe I'll be asleep when she comes.'

'Oh no, you won't,' I smirk. 'I'll tell her you're pretending.'

'Hello! It's Jasmine is it?' The chaplain is a thin woman in an ivory suit jacket. Her clothes match her hair which hangs straight to her shoulders in a long bob. She smiles and her mouth is small and not very stretchy.

'Yes,' Jay says. She only sort of smiles, but at least she doesn't *sound* sulky.

'And I'm Emily, her older sister.' I step forward with a proper smile. 'Would you like a chair? Here.'

'Oh, yes please. Lovely.' The chaplain perches on the edge of the plastic. 'I saw you a little while ago, didn't I Jasmine? I think I met your mum?'

'Yeah,' Jay nods. 'She's not here today.'

'How nice to have your sister then!' the chaplain coos.

Jay nods without looking at me. I imagine 'nice' isn't quite the word she has in mind. I drag up another chair, so that I'm sitting just a bit behind the bed. Far enough that the chaplain can't help but address most of the conversation to Jay, but close enough that in a different setting I might be mistaken as a bouncer. Then again, I'm five foot three, so maybe not.

I wait. The chaplain smiles at Jasmine again. Is she going to continue the conversation? Her mouth twitches. Yes. No. Yes! 'Here. I brought some, um, colouring books.' She pulls a floppy book from her large purse and places it on Jay's knees.

'Oh! Thank you.'

I twist my neck. It's the sort of book you'd give a six year old: Chunkily outlined clowns and dogs with bows. I wince. However old she looks, Jay's records definitely say she's sixteen. More silence. Jay fiddles with the colouring book and then finally looks up. The chaplain smiles again. Silence.

'Er, how has your day been?' It's Jay asking. If I was her parent I'd be proud. What's the chaplain doing? Even I can maintain small talk longer than this.

'Oh! Good. Well, busy.' The chaplain leans forward. 'How are you?'

'Okay.'

'You've had an operation haven't you?'

Maybe the chaplain doesn't get a copy of the patient's notes? Then again, she came last week so she should remember something...

'Yeah, another one.' Jay rather graciously gives her a conversational lead.

'Oh. When do you go home then?' Ouch. Not the right question.

'Dunno. When CSF stops leaking out of my nose.'

'Oh.' The chaplain does a sort of wiggle. 'I'm sorry.'

'It's okay.' Jay falls silent.

'No, it sounds awful.'

What's she supposed to say to that? *Yes, it* feels *awful too?* Jay begins to stroke her cannula. 'It's okay.' I wince.

'I'm sorry.' the chaplain persists.

Jay raises her head. 'No, really it's fine. It doesn't hurt that much today.'

'Oh. Good.'

'I had a good sleep last night too.' Jay offers. I thought the chaplain was supposed to be cheering Jasmine up, not the other way around.

'Oh. Good.' More silence.

'And you know. God is in control.' Jay keeps her voice casual. Am I the only one who can sense an underlying irritation?

'Oh. Yes... Yes.'

'Finally. I thought she'd be here all day.' Jay kicks her legs. The colouring book slides off the sheet and slithers across the floor.

'Jay.' I try for a reproving tone, but can't put any heart into it. I leave the book where it is.

Jay crosses her arms. 'I don't want to see her again.'

'Maybe she was just nervous? Perhaps she was having a bad day?'

'I had to try and make *her* feel better!'

I sigh. 'Why was she so bad at talking?'

'Do you believe me now?'

I nod and sigh again. 'Yeah. Sorry. It's so frustrating though. She had the chance to share God's love and comfort and instead…' Instead I'm going to have to try and fulfil that role. It would have been such a relief to palm it off to someone else. Jay might see me as an ally now, but I'm under no delusions that she's going to open up her heart to me and let me walk beside her. I'm under no delusions that this is even something I'm capable of doing. *Oh Lord, send someone else.*

Tears in the night

DIARY EXCERPT
September 23, 2015 (9 days in hospital)

Last night was hard. We got a call that Jasmine's drain had broken, become de-sterilized, and she might have to have a third operation. They began fasting her for it. That was terrible. I was so, so tired but for the first time in the fortnight felt really, really sad. I wanted to cry but I was too tired.

I had a disrupted sleep with weird dreams but woke in the morning to discover that all was well. [They've fixed the drain.] No operation for the time being.

Chapter Nine: Life Interrupted

'**G**atsby believed in the green light, the orgastic future that year by year recedes before us. It eluded us then, but that's no matter—tomorrow we will run faster, stretch out our arms farther. . . . And one fine morning – So we beat on, boats against the current, borne back ceaselessly into the past." I close the book with a snap. 'There. Done!'

Normally I'd linger over those last, poetic lines, but after two weeks of reading and suffering – Jasmine in having to listen to that much of my voice, me in having to re-read chapters each time she fell asleep, which happened with frustrating frequency – I'm just thankful we've reached the final page intact. 'Do you think you could write an essay on it?' I ask.

'Nope.'

I resist the urge to sigh. 'Let's go through the themes. You write them down and we'll find quotes together.'

She looks at me and wiggles her fingers. I sigh. I keep forgetting. Since her second operation she hasn't been allowed to sit any higher than twenty degrees off horizontal. No walking. Washing, toileting and eating are time-consuming and messy. Writing is impossible.

'Okay, *I'll* write.' I pull an exercise book from my bag with a flourish – here's what I prepared earlier – and drag the rolling table over so it bashes into my knees. 'The key themes are death, love, time, money—'

'Money?'

'Remember? The difference between the people with new money living on West Egg coast, and the old, inherited fortunes of those on East Egg.'

She stares, her blank look asking 'Have we read the same book?' Well we *have*, because we've read it *together*. For *hours*.

'Eggs?' She's sniggering.

I do sigh this time. Today is the date of her original discharge. The day her HSC year starts. The day the rest of her peers leave her behind. 'Right,' I interrupt before she can make some inane comment on chickens. 'Let's discuss symbols. Can you think of any?'

She shifts in bed. 'I'm thirsty.'

I put the exercise book down and get up to fill her cup. 'How about the green light?' I ask when I return.

'The green light?'

'Are you going to repeat everything I say?' I hold the cup and bend the straw to an appropriate angle. 'I just read it, remember?'

'Stop getting cranky at me.' Her lips find the straw and she sips.

'I'm not getting cranky... okay.' I sit down and pick up the pen. 'Sorry. Now what other symbols can you think of?'

She stares at the painted balloons on the wall. I wonder if she's the first patient in the children's ward to begin their HSC while hospitalised. Probably. They normally kick you into the adults' section at sixteen. Her seventeenth birthday is in less than a month. She'll be home and we'll eat cake together and –

'Umm...'

Before she can say the wrong answer – I think I'll cry if she does – I give it to her. 'The billboard.'

'What billboard?'

'The one with the picture of the man wearing glasses? Dr. T. J. Eckleburg.'

'He's a billboard?' She stares in consternation. 'I thought he was real. One of the characters.'

'He's an advertisement.' I say. I'm not sure if she's going to laugh or cry. I'm not sure if *I'm* going to laugh or cry. Then she closes her eyes.

'I don't want to do any more.'

'How about we make a list of themes and then –'

'No.'

'Look you don't have to do your HSC this year,' I say. 'Mum rung the school yesterday. There are so many options.' I can see the mountain of work she has ahead of her, and it looks nigh on impossible from this vantage point. The flush of achievement from finishing *The Great Gatsby* suddenly feels insignificant. 'The hospital is more than happy to write you—'

'No!' Her eyes are open again. 'I want to graduate with my friends! I'm not staying behind.' She crosses her arms, readjusting her cannula as though it's a blue-bottle with stingers still attached. She's a very experienced wrangler.

'Fine.' I match her glare easily. 'You can do that. *I really think you can*, whatever they say. I'll tutor you. I'll do everything *I* can, but it's going to be hard, and you'll have to really put in the effort.'

'I *am* putting in the effort,' she grumbles, and I know she's going to give up in the face of the challenge. She always has. I remember a paragraph from the brain tumour information booklet. *People with brain tumours can exhibit listlessness, lack of motivation and fatigue. This can present as laziness to those around them. Lack of appropriate hormones can result in mood swings and emotional compromise.*

Before I can respond, before I can offer her an easy escape, her expression changes. There's determination in it now, and something I've never seen before, a hungry sort of drive, a flicker of steel. She leans back in bed. 'If Dr. Whatever-his-name is a symbol you'd better write him down,' she concedes.

I gape at this glimpse into hidden fires, depths to her character, obscured until now. For the first time I wonder who she might have been, if at birth the tumour had not begun its ravenous conquest.

Then, I wonder who she might still become.

'Jasmine! It's your endocrinologist.'

The voice comes from behind the blue curtains which are closed and tucked around her bed cubicle. We look in its direction and then at each other. Jasmine's on the green bedpan. I'm sitting beside her with clean tissues.

'Just a minute!' I call.

The curtains sway. A hand appears, about to pull them back. I drop my cloth and hurry around the bed. Will I make it? The blue barricade trembles.

'Wait!' I leap forward, and with a twist I'm quite proud of, manage to slip out of the cubicle while keeping the curtains firmly closed. I even avoid a direct collision with the owner of the hand. 'Jasmine's having a bath.'

The lunch lady holds up a plastic food tray.

Another hand sets the curtains trembling. We look at each other. 'Honestly, everyone comes at the wrong time,' Jasmine mutters.

'You should have a sign.'

'Isn't that what closed curtains are?'

We snigger. 'She's getting her drain checked!' I call.

The hand departs.

'Hello Jasmine. I'm Timothy, your new nurse for this afternoon. I just need to run through a few housekeeping bits and pieces...'

Jay waits patiently as he checks her allergies, birthday, number of drains and time of last pain relief. I stare ferociously into the corner. He straightens and tucks away his papers. 'Er... one last thing.' He looks at Jasmine and then away quickly. 'If you need help going to the... toilet.' What a lovely word for the plastic potty she has to use while lying on her back. 'Feel free to er... call a female nurse.'

He leaves and I burst into laughter. 'Poor man. His face!'

'Ow! Don't make my drain hurt!' Jasmine laughs too.

'Do you think he always looks like that?' I whisper.

'Permanently shocked?'

'Like a cartoon character whose face has been frozen?'

'Naww,' Jay visibly attempts to conjure sympathy. She's a better woman than I. 'He can't help it.'

'I know.' I capture my laughter for a second. 'But I couldn't look at him, I knew I would giggle. It's just… funny?'

We snicker with our hands over our mouths like ten-year-olds. We can't stop for ages, and it feels good.

'She can sit up now.'

'Really?' In my astonishment I look Timothy full in the face. Bad idea. *Retreat!* I bite my lip.

The nurse nods. Despite his raised eyebrows and long face, he's not the joking type. Trust me, we've tried. 'I rang the team. They believe the leak in her nose will have healed by now. The lumbar drain has slowed right down; we'll take it out tomorrow.'

'I won't start leaking CSF again?' Jasmine picks at her cannula.

'It will have healed by now,' he repeats. 'You can sit up to ninety degrees, but no walking.' He leaves and I jump to my feet.

'Yay! Finally.'

Jasmine grins but I can tell she's still worried. 'Go on, press the button.'

'Are you sure...?'

'Yes.' I'm impatient now. 'If you want to get out of here you need to sit up.'

That does it. *Eeep*. The bed groans as it raises its head. 'I'm sitting!'

'I can see that.' Now she's caught my excitement, I switch back to cool and calm. *Someone* has to have their feet firmly on the ground.

'Ooh the ward looks bigger from this angle —oh!' Her joy turns to pain. 'Oh, my head! It *hurts*. I feel sick... I'm going to—'

I plunge my finger on the down button of the bed control and root for a clean vomit bag with my free hand. 'Here!'

She retches for a while. I rub her shoulder until she shakes me off. 'Too hot!'

'Poor thing.'

'It's the change in pressure,' Timothy explains minutes later. 'Perhaps I can find something for the nausea.'

Perhaps? 'That's a very good idea,' I say.

By the time I go to leave, Jay's feeling slightly better. 'I'm having dinner with a friend tonight.' I mumble, gathering my belongings, hunting for my phone. 'Otherwise I could have stayed for a few more hours.'

'That'll be fun!' Jasmine sounds excited. I hadn't mentioned it until now in case she felt left out. 'Where are you going?'

I shrug. 'Dunno.' I don't really care. I'm tired and don't feel like going out. Perhaps I'll cancel. Social situations are difficult now. If I don't mention Jasmine I feel like a liar. If I do, it's an instant downer.

'Enjoy!' She gives me a bright smile.

Who knew sitting up for 0.7 seconds could be so elating? Maybe I should give it a try.

Unexpected joys

DIARY EXCERPT
September 27, 2015 (12 days in hospital)

In the evening I was going out with a friend for dinner to celebrate my birthday. My whole family was unusually supportive of the idea, to the extent that Mum tried to do my hair with water and leave-in conditioner - to no avail, it's untameable. Her final advice was this: either wear a hat or go stand in the wind!

I thought it was because I hadn't really been anywhere but the hospital for two weeks. Walking into the restaurant my friend led me over to a table for ten... and I was absolutely stomverbaasd! [Note: Dutch for gobsmacked] Friends from school and church and beach mission with balloons and cake and presents. For me!

I couldn't believe they'd actually thought so much about my birthday. I still can't believe it. Such, *such* love. I'm so humbled. I don't deserve it, and I certainly didn't expect it. There are some things in life which are nice but you can do without, and you're used to doing without and you're content with doing without, because so little in life is strictly necessary.

And then, sometimes, those things happen. Unneeded, unsought, but absolutely delightful. A breath of sweet wind. And life for a little while just takes on that shiny edge, and you feel *special.*

Chapter Ten: It's a Complicated War

I wander downstairs. Dad's at the computer. Silver splinters dance across the wooden floor from the vertical blinds. 'Mmm.' It's too early to formulate words.

I try again once I emerge from the toilet. 'How're you?'

'Tired.'

'Didn't sleep well?'

Dad rotates round on the office chair. He's wearing a rumpled navy t-shirt and grey shorts. 'Woke early. Five.'

I move towards the coffee mugs. I'll need a strong cuppa if I'm to fill out another job application before the breakfast youth leaders' meeting. I hate applying for jobs – but it keeps everyone happy. It reassures those at church that I have a life outside of the hospital, and reminds Mum and Dad they only have one daughter to worry about.

There's only a few weeks left of uni. Three years done and dusted. I wish I had the brain space to be excited. I will soon! If Jasmine's medical teams give the 'OK' today, discharge will follow. I can't wait. 'Why didn't you try and go back to sleep?'

Dad rubs his unshaven chin. The computer screen baptises his grey hair eerie blue. 'I couldn't. Thinking about Jasmine.'

I swallow. He looks awful. 'You can't do anything, you know. We can only pray.'

He shakes his head. 'I haven't stopped.'

The rasping of his voices stops *me*. I stand in the shadowy dining room, mug in hand, and feel helpless. My Dad does not do emotion. Yet since all this began, it seems, he does. I have nothing to say. To watch your youngest daughter suffer like this… suddenly I realise I've got the easier card. I'm just the sister. I didn't forge Jasmine out of love and biology and mystery. I didn't cradle her when she was small, *I* was too busy trying to find a place to read away from her toddler screams. Lord, bring her home today. Even if it's just for Dad, please. I don't know how much longer he can—

Derrr derrr. Derrr derrr. We jump. Dad looks at me. I raise my free hand in abdication. *I'm* not getting it.

He sighs, and lumbers for the handset. 'Hello, Paul speaking.'

Silence.

'Oh, hello.'

I know immediately it's the hospital.

I cry and then I get dressed and walk to the breakfast meeting.

'Hey!'

'Morning Emily.'

'Hello, Em.'

'Hi, friend.' The last speaker gives me a hug. Then the question of the day (week, month?): 'How's your sister?'

I take a deep breath and look around the sunny kitchen. The table is laid with pancake toppings and orange juice and an incongruously American jug of purple kool-aid. There's about seven of us: both genders, varying ages, varying life experiences. Married. With kids. Single.

Just talk. Don't think about what you're staying. It's a beautiful day outside. Flitting sunshine and blue sky. Dancing trees and sweet air. 'They rang this morning,' I begin. There's no need to explain who 'they' are. 'Her nose began leaking in the night. They're fasting her.' I don't meet any eyes. 'They're going to operate again.' My voice is going to descend into a wobble any second. 'Mum's sick but they need someone to sign the consent. I'll go after this and Dad will drive with Mum later.'

'Oh no!'

'That's awful news.'

'I'm sorry.'

'Oh, Em.'

I wipe my eyes. 'Sorry. Thought I was done crying.'

'Hey Jay!'

'I'm fasting.' A miserable, pale face.

'I know.' I pull the curtains closed around us. 'It sucks.'

'I can taste it, you know. The CSF in the back of my throat.'

'Yeah?'

She wiggles her nose. 'It's sort of salty.'

I sit down beside her bed. 'When did you begin fasting?'

'After breakfast!' There's more, I can tell. I wait. 'I thought I could taste it during the night,' she continues, 'and definitely early this morning, but they had to do the test, you know?'

'I know.'

'So they sent off the sample, and a nurse told me I could eat. I didn't want to, but I was hungry and she said I could!' Jay pounds the bed in frustration. 'Now I have to wait until the afternoon because it has to be on an empty stomach.' Her hand slides off the sheets. 'I'm thirsty.'

There's nothing to say. I go to her bedside table and hunt around. 'I could read your second English text.'

'No!'

'It would pass the time.' I urge. 'Think how good it would be if we finished half of it before the op.'

She bursts into tears.

'Okay, okay, I'm sorry.' I shove the book away. I'm never sure whether to humour her or persist. At least on operation days I don't feel the need to play bad cop. 'Let's play I Spy.'

'I can't see.' She pouts.

'That's because you're crying.' I sit back down and study the room. Any new object would be too easy a guess, but we've run through the permanent fixtures multiple times already. Time to get tricky. 'I spy with my little eye something that starts with 'W'.'

She sniffs, face red and blotchy. 'Wood?'

'Nope.' I look covertly at the clock. Five hours to go.

'Watch!'

I glance at my wrist. 'No.'

'Ummm...' she begins to, well, not exactly 'cheer up', but look less glum. 'W – W – W – Wedding!'

'Do you see a wedding?' I ask, waving an arm, 'in here?'

'There could be one outside...'

I roll my eyes. 'Yes, hospital car park, prime spot for wedding photography.'

She giggles and gazes around the room, interest in the game renewed. 'Umm… Water?'

'Yes!'

Her eyes fill with tears. 'I want water,' she moans. 'I'm so, so thirsty.'

Whoops. 'You can have ice.'

'I don't want ice! It's not the same.'

I sit back down. 'Did you sleep well last night?'

'No,' she grumbles, 'my nose was leaking.'

'How about you have a rest then?' I suggest brightly. 'Who knows, you might sleep until the surgery.'

'Don't want to sleep.'

Well, I don't want to think of any more ideas. So there.

'Where's Mum?'

'She's sick, you know that.' I don't like it when she asks for Mum. It's a reminder that, try as I might, I can never be everything Jay needs. 'You spoke to her on the phone this morning. She'd be here if she could.'

'I want her.'

'She'll be here by the time you come out of surgery.' I say. 'Now are you sure you don't want me to read your English text?' It's a last, desperate attempt. I think I like that book even less than Jasmine does, although I've never let on. I didn't study it myself and Google hasn't been particularly enlightening. Besides, it's a difficult book to read out loud, full of non-English words, place-names, and encounters between people which seem to go nowhere.

'No.' She's gone quiet, staring at the ceiling. 'My head hurts. I'm hungry.'

'I know! I *know* you're in pain and hungry and thirsty, and I *know* it must feel like—'

'KNOW?' she bellows, all quietness gone. 'Know? You don't know anything! How can you *possibly* know?'

I stare at her, horror-struck, because she's right. How *can* I know? She glares through tears of fury. I have no tears, but if I did, they would be of shame and guilt. 'I'm going to the toilet.' I manage.

When I return my temper is under control. I think. 'I'm sorry,' I say and my voice breaks. 'You're right. I can't know. I can't know at all. But at the same time, I'm just trying to help and you're not being very…' This is the way all my apologies seem to go. It's like knitting an unravelling scarf. The explanations end up somehow cancelling out the 'sorry'. Today, I manage to stop just before I reach the last inch of wool. Today it *is* an apology.

Of sorts.

When the doctors come in with the consent form I have to stop myself from leaping up and snatching it out of their hands. 'Emily, isn't it?'

'Yes.' They don't ask how old I am, but this act of neglect brings no thrill. Not today. My backside is numb, my head aches and I never, *ever,* want to play I Spy again. *Please let this be the last operation. Surely three is enough?* I look over at Jasmine and she closes her eyes in relief.

I sign the paperwork.

Organising takes forever but eventually the wardsman arrives and the nurses transfer the drips and drains from the stands to the bed.

Down the hall, into the lift. Jay whimpers as her bed goes over a bump. I walk by her side. Down another corridor. The wardsman presses a button. Jasmine's eyes are shut in pain. Double doors swing open and we go in.

This is part of the hospital I haven't seen before. It's set up like a sort of lounge room. There's a box of toys in the corner, and a huge Banana-in-Pyjamas plushie. Winnie-the-Pooh dances across the TV screen. The nurse wanders off to talk to the surgery staff, a sheaf of notes under her arm. The wardsman flicks a glance to the TV, where Winnie-the-Pooh has got himself covered in honey, and leaves.

'Want a toy?' I tease. 'I can get you a teddy bear.'

'I'm good.'

'Really?' I trip across to the toy box. 'You don't even want a...' I pick up the first stuffed thing I can find, '...monkey?'

'Okay,' she says unexpectedly. Trapped by my own joke, I have no choice but to bring it over.

'Are you okay?'

'Yes.' Her eyes blaze with unbirthed dread. Her lip wobbles.

'Are you sure?' I take her hand but it's unresponsive, a deflated balloon.

'Am I going to die?' She begins to cry.

'No!' I rear back, horrified. 'At least, the doctors don't think so,' I add, for honesty's sake. 'You *know* they have to mention all the possible risks when they do the consent. They make it sound terrifying, but—'

'I want Mum.'

'I know.' I try and hug her. The bed rails make it awkward, an all too obvious reminder that any moment now she will be taken where I can't follow. 'I love you Jay. Jesus loves you too.'

'I'm scared.'

'He's got you in his hands.' I chatter mindlessly until the nurse returns with reinforcements. If she notices Jasmine's tear-streaked face, she doesn't say a thing.

'Do you want to walk in?' She makes it sound like she's offering a treat: I know you have to have your head cut open, but if you like you can stroll into the theatre all by yourself!'

'I'm not allowed to walk.' Jay's eyes dart around the room, daunted by this departure from status quo.

'It's hardly going to matter if your nose leaks now,' I say.

'You can walk,' a theatre nurse agrees.

Jay nods. I can read her trepidation in the stiff way she climbs down from the bed, but she doesn't say a word. They give us blue booties and head caps, and putting them on is the closest I will ever get to walking in her shoes, to 'knowing'. Is there anywhere else on earth where the division between Health and Sickness is so obvious? In ten minutes I'll stroll out and chuck my disposables in the bin. Probably make myself a coffee. Eat. I'm starving because I didn't want to eat while she was fasting. In a few hours she'll be rolled out, unconscious, and for the third time the healing process will begin from square one.

I grip her hand as tightly as she grips mine. We enter the operating theatre. 'I don't want to!' Jay breaks down. The anaesthetist comes up with a smile. They run through the mandatory pre-surgery checks. Correct girl. Correct surgery. Jay lies down on the padded black table. She's trembling, one tiny step away from absolutely losing it.

'It's going to be okay,' I continue my running, murmuring dialogue, trying to be calming, trying to be truthful. I never promise her she is not going to die.

'You're in good hands, I know you're scared. It will be all over soon.'

Her eyes dart wildly around, and all of a sudden I catch the contagion. I, who've been in countless operating theatres as a student. I, for whom the hulking roof-high machines hold no mystery. I, ...am *terrified*.

She's crying on the bed, tears pooling in her ears, and I have to turn my face away, because a tear is coming out of my right eye.

'Now breathe in deeply.' They cover her face with a mask. 'Another breath.'

Jay snaps. 'Nooo!' She wails, bucking and scrabbling at the mask. She tears it off. The anaesthetist pulls it back up. I reach over and pin her down against the bed, crying. 'Help! No! I don't want to dieee!'

I long to throw myself over her body and protect it from the surgeon's knife, the unnatural gas, the fearful unknown. She calls to me for help but I push her shoulders firmly to the bed and swallow my bile. I am Judas. I am Brutus. I am Emily.

At last she sags. I sag too, first away from her seemingly lifeless body, and then out the door and as far away from the operating theatre as possible. I give myself a few minutes and then pick up my phone to call Dad. I know what he meant now, when he said she fought the anaesthetic.

I feel like I've survived a war, and I would be relieved, except none of this feels like winning.

Chapter Eleven: The Weight of Other People

I meander into Mum's bedroom the next morning and watch her reconnect her insulin pump. 'It was awful seeing her struggle against the anaesthetic,' I say. 'Really awful.'

Mum looks up. 'I can't believe she's had three operations. It all feels like a dream.'

If it's a dream, it must be a nightmare. I grimace and look out the window at the huddled bush and the stretching tree branches. 'I can go in today if you want.'

'I'm going.'

'Are you sure? You've been so sick lately. You should rest.' I'm sensible, calm, coherent – and doing a pretty good job of it, considering my insides are roiling like one of J. M. Turner's oil paint storms.

'She's my daughter.' Mum runs a comb through her shower-damp hair. 'I want to go. I'm going.'

'Okay.' I can't bring myself to say any more. 'Give her my love.'

As soon as the garage door winds down and I hear her car changing from *reverse* to *drive* I wander into the kitchen. I feel numb. Job applications can wait. Everything can wait. I pull the tub of my birthday ice-cream from the freezer and fetch a spoon.

No one ever told me sadness could be so physical. I've seen a lot of odd x-rays as a radiography student, but one trumps them all. A person swallowed a tree seed and it grew inside their lungs, suffocating them with oxygen hungry pine needles. That's what this sadness felt like. As though my entire chest cavity is being smothered by an unruly plant which wants *out*. Except there is no 'out', no place to go.

When my grandparents died it was different, because my sadness was allowed to peter out with my memory of them. When I watch my mum struggle it is different again, because she's *always* struggled. I've never known any better. Familiarity hasn't bred contempt so much as resignation. Yet my sister's sadness-bush grows and grows.

I carry it around inside me, and its weight has become normal, so much so, that I often forget about it. Yet on days like this, after nights like that, I can feel it unfurling new branches, sending out deeper and deeper roots. If you took an x-ray of my chest would you see it? What shape would the woody branches form, spreading out from deep under my diaphragm to the apices of my lungs? A cross-like shape would be beautifully symbolic.

Knowing my luck, it looks like a deformed bird's nest. I cry, I eat ice-cream in front of the computer, and I am grateful for the reprieve.

Ding dong.

The doorbell. I wipe my face and trek up the stairs. A quick peek through the window. 'Oh, hello!'

Fishing the door keys out of Jasmine's joggers – who dropped them there? – I pull open the wooden door. 'Hello! One sec...' I get the screen door open.

'Emily! How are you? I brought a meal. Nothing fancy. Chicken pasta. And some biscuits.' A smile, a wink, a considering sweep of the eyes... and my arms are full of warm casserole dish. The aluminium smell of foil mixes with the rich scent of roast chicken.

'Yum! Thank you so much. We really appreciate it.' I try and meet her eyes properly, this lady from church, and somehow convey the gratitude and helplessness I cannot express. She's not the first to drop a meal, and the roster pinned to our calendar tells me she won't be the last. 'It's so wonderful to just be able to heat something up when we get back late.' I say.

She smiles and brushes the words away with a hand. 'I was so sad to hear about the third operation. Couldn't believe it.' A shake of the head. 'And how are you?'

'Okay. Just tired.' I smile and lean against the doorframe and my sadness-bush retreats just a little under the weight of her eyes.

She leans forward and hugs me around the hot dish. 'We're praying. We're all praying. It's hard to know what God's got planned, but he works all things for his good, you know?'

I nod. She stands there for a second longer. 'Look after yourself.'

'I will.' I'm not sure what I'm agreeing to, but I know it's the right answer. 'Thanks again!' I wave one-handedly and deposit the ceramic dish on the stairs before closing the door.

There's something beautiful and painful about accepting meals and gifts. It's humbling and God-glorifying and sometimes I simply don't know what to say. I pray the people who knock at the door understand.

I think they do.

'And how's Jas going spiritually?'

I sigh beneath my borrowed hat and squint out at the thirty degree sun as Maria pushes her toddler stroller up the hill. She's hit the jackpot. Finally someone's dared to ask the question which has been haunting me. Pity I have no million dollars to give.

'I don't know.' I clench my fists and my calves tighten and stretch as I propel myself up the incline. Even without a bulky stroller it's a tough walk. 'I – she said something really cool after the second surgery. She said the 'good' God is working is the love of our church family. I – I couldn't believe it… She's never said anything like that before. She just doesn't seem to think that deeply.'

'That's really special.'

'Yeah.' I peel my t-shirt away from my neck and flap the collar. There's no breeze. 'But without the drugs she doesn't want to talk about it. Every time I bring it up, she shuts me down. I don't know what to do.' I'm failing her.

My friend hums. I lengthen my strides. We reach the top of the hill and breathe. Eucalyptus scented air meanders through our sweat-soaked hair. Somewhere in the valley below a dog barks. I'm afraid. These are dangerous surgeries. If Jay dies—

'Is she tired?'

'Yeah. She falls asleep at random times all day. And I get that thinking deeply is hard when you're like that. But she's *never* wanted to talk about this sort of stuff. It…' I blink at the unclouded sky. 'It worries me.'

We walk on in silence. I can tell my friend is thinking, and as she does something unusual happens. Each step without speech seems to confer more value to my fears. Instead of being awkward remnants of abstract theology, they become concrete concerns. My questions are serious puzzle-pieces, her silence promises, but they will form a picture. It's a reassuring benediction.

'I think,' she says finally, 'that the time will come. Everyone reaches a point in their lives when they want to talk about deeper, spiritual things. You, maybe earlier than others. Your sister, maybe a bit later.'

I wait.

'Right now you are showing her that you are a safe person. You are with her in hospital. You haven't left her in her pain, or when she's frustrated or tired. You're showing you can be trusted. That's all you can do. When the time comes, she'll seek you out.' A burbling noise rises from the stroller. 'Or perhaps she won't. That is in God's hands. But all you can do is what you are doing. Nothing is wasted. You're showing her you are safe.'

Safe. I like the thought of that, if only because it casts a glamour over what is my extraordinarily unglamorous life at the moment. 'Showing Jasmine I'm a safe person' sounds much better than 'sitting by the bed and resisting the urge to throttle my sick sister'.

I'm not the right person for this.

Derr. Derr. Derr. I race upstairs. Is it the hospital? Someone from church? Dad from work? Surely Mum would ring my mobile. I dive to the floor of my parent's room and snatch up the landline before it stops. Just in time.

'Hello-this-is-Emily.' My heart is thumping so loudly from the sprint I have to hold the receiver away from my ear to hear properly.

'Hello Ma'am, I'm ringing up about a survey. Are you the homeowner?'

A shot of Relief. A deluge of Frustration. 'No sorry—'

'Are you over eighteen?'

'Yes, but—' I pull the handset even further away from my ear.

'I have a survey, just a few questions. Five minutes—'

'Sorry, not interested.'

'Please Ma'am. Most important—'

Important? He thinks *this* is important? I clap the phone back to my ear. 'NO!' I shout. 'No, I *cannot* do a survey! My sister is in hospital with a brain tumour and—' My voice buckles, as it does every time I say those two words: brain tumour. My own inescapable Pavlovian reflex. I hate it. 'And... *No!*'

I slam the phone down and burst into tears.

Chapter Twelve: Chocolate and Vampire Toenails

'Hey hey!' I bustle into the ward with bags hanging from my shoulders and falling off my wrists. 'It's me. Traffic was horrendous as usual. Goodness, I need coffee.' I dump my load and come around to the front of the bed. I examine her face. 'You slept well?'

Jay smiles and holds out her arms. 'Morning.'

I stoop to squeeze her gently. 'You didn't throw up again?'

'Nope.' She smiles proudly. It's clear she did sleep well for once. Probably helps that her ward-mates have been transferred and she has the four-bed room to herself again. 'And my water didn't run out until 6 am.'

'Good!' Experience has taught me that a sixteen-year-old who's been up since 3 am drinking because her water hormones have worn out does not pleasant company make.

'And...' she rolls the word with the expertise of a girl who did drama as a school elective, '... they're going to remove one of my drains today!'

'So good!' I crow, fishing the snap lock bag of instant coffee from my handbag. 'It's just as well if you're coming home in a week. Do you want anything from the kitchen?'

'There's some cheese in a bag. It's got my name on it.'

I place my stained styrofoam cup on the rolling table and begin my daily routine of Throwing Things Away. 'Finished with this?' I collect the unused plastic cutlery into a pile. If it's still here when Mum comes to visit it will make a re-appearance in our kitchen at home. She's a firm advocate of Waste Not Want Not. I blame her immigrant upbringing but I'm determined not to inherit it. 'And this?' I hold up a jelly cup. 'Want it?'

Jay shrugs. 'Not really.' Before she can protest I add it to my pile and head towards the bin.

'Now,' I say as I return, plopping myself down onto the plastic-covered bedside chair and gathering my bags towards me, 'I'll show you what I've brought –'

'Ah, hello!' A familiar nurse enters, bearing Jasmine's notes and a big smile. 'Perfect timing!' She moves over to the bed. 'What a good big sister you have! Did she bring these chocolates?' She waves at a beautiful box on the shelf above Jasmine's bed.

'No, they're from my friends.'

'And how much have you drunk this morning?' The nurse sweeps on. 'The last thing I've got on the list is half a cup of orange juice.'

Jasmine lists her fluid intake. 170 millilitres in a standard styrofoam cup. 150 millilitres in a bottle of milk. She knows the measurements off by heart.

'Wonderful.' The nurse lifts her pen off the page. 'And pain-wise?'

'Okay.' Jasmine shifts. 'Got a bit of a headache.'

'Panadol's due in an hour.' The nurse considers. 'Do you think you can hold off 'till then? You're already on the strong stuff, so I can't give it any earlier.'

'It's okay.'

'And no leaking?'

The crucial question. 'I don't think so.'

The nurse frowns.

'I mean, not that I know of.' Jay flaps her hands. 'I can't taste anything at the back of my throat.' She closes her mouth and concentrates. 'At least, I don't think…'

'Good, let's keep it that way.' The nurse puts her notes down on the rolling table. 'Because you, sugarplum, are going to have a shower!'

'I am?' Jasmine looks at her sideways, as if she can hardly bear to hope she's hearing the truth.

'Yep. Your sister can help you. We'll get a wheelchair.' Jasmine looks uncertain, probably worried her spinal fluid will start leaking again as soon as she stands. 'Don't tell me you want another bed-bath?'

'No!' Desire overcomes Hesitancy. Then Hesitancy stages a comeback tour. Jasmine flutters her long thin hands again. 'If you're sure…'

'Positive.' The nurse eyes the catheter bag. 'I'll empty that first so you don't have to lug it around with you, and then the doctor will come to take out your lumbar drain. After that… bath time!'

Beep. Beep. Beep.

'Nargh. There it goes again. Try not to put pressure on your foot.'

'And how,' Jasmine retorts, 'am I supposed to walk then?'

'Hop? Get better arm veins?'

She rolls her eyes and limps over to the wheelchair, cannulated foot sticking out in front like a courting peacock.

'Wait,' I hold the handles steady and prise up the footrests. 'There. Watch out!' I snatch the drip stand which is supposed to be coming with us before it can escape down the corridor. 'I think I need more hands.'

'I think I need a sleep.' Jay sags back in the wheelchair with a muffled moan. It was three steps from bed to chair, and that's more than she's taken in a month.

'Your head?'

She nods with her eyes closed. 'The pressure.'

'Ready?' I wait for her grin. 'Onwards!'

Rattle Rattle Rattle. 'Stop! You're going too fast!'

'This is a perfectly normal pace.' *Riiiip*.

'Is something caught in my wheels?'

'The shower's down the end right?'

'I think that was my gown.'

Beep. Beep. Beep comes from the drip stand. 'There goes your foot again.'

'Oooh, don't turn so suddenly. My head!'

'Whoops.' I brake in front of the shower. Almost missed it. 'Er, here we are?' We stare at the single door, wide enough to admit one wheelchair and… nothing else.

'Perhaps if I push the drip stand in front of me…' But no, the footrests jut too far out and her arms are too short. 'Maybe if I push you in, and then turn and grab it…' This time it's the drip line that's not long enough. 'Who invents these places?'

Jasmine's tiring fast. We haven't even got inside the bathroom yet. I eye the stand with its draping lines and flapping fluid bags. 'You put your catheter bag on your lap, and I'll carry the stand over the threshold and push you in with my knees.' I'm met with a sceptical face. It says: *Look Emily, I know you do karate, but honestly…*

My plan works, and there's only one fraction of a second in which it looks like we're going to tear her remaining drains out. A success all round. Minutes later the nurse appears with clean towels, another gown, and toiletries. She looks at us both, is apparently happy with whatever it is she sees, (two people who have no clue what they're doing?) and retreats with the advice to 'not get the drain or stitch sites too wet.'

Sounds easy enough.

I look at Jasmine and then away. 'Er, are you sure you're happy for me to…' I give her a vague wave. 'The nurse will do it if you ask.'

'It's fine,' she says. Her flushed cheeks, evidence of the exciting nature of our adventures thus far, are beginning to pale. We'll have to be quick. I help her undress. The catheter and drip present a challenge.

'It's that way around.'

'No, it's this way.'

'It's *my* catheter! Put it through the shorts first.'

'Okay, fine! Oh. I can't believe that worked.' All too soon she's naked in the shower chair, sitting on a spare towel ('Can you imagine how many other people have sat here?' 'I'm sure they clean it.' 'I'm not having a shower unless you put a towel there first.').

I wait for it to be awkward. My little sister, all scars and bruises and betadine stains. Child-like skin. Experienced eyes. But it feels normal. A bit sad, yes, but not weird. 'Right, let's do this.' I look at the soaps the nurse left us. Tiny bottles, reminiscent of the ones you collect from hotels. 'This looks like baby-stuff. You're going to come out of here smelling like talcum powder and old ladies.'

She giggles. 'It's hypoallergenic. And there's nothing wrong with old ladies.'

'There is if you're sixteen.'

I'm soaking wet by the time we finish. It's not easy washing someone on a chair, while avoiding surgical dressings and trying to de-tangle hair which has been rubbed against bed sheets for four weeks straight.

'Ow! You're hurting me.'

'This is what *I* do with *my* hair.'

'You don't have any hair!'

'I do too. I'll have you know it's almost reaching my earlobes.'

Jasmine snorts. 'Careful,' she pleads. 'You're yanking it.'

'I'm not *trying* to. Think of it as character building.'

'Perhaps it's more character building for you to learn how to brush hair properly!'

We make it back to her bed at last. I need a second coffee. 'Chocolate time!'

'Okay,' Jay agrees. 'Can you reach it?'

I topple the box of chocolates from the shelf.

'I don't like the white ones,' she says.

Nice try. 'I don't either.'

'Dad'll eat them.'

We each take a milk. I suck mine while searching through her cupboard. 'Where's your English text?'

She smirks. 'I hid it.'

I pull open her desk drawer. 'And I found it.' Flopping onto the vinyl chair I put my feet up on her bed. Ah. It's much easier now she's not so sensitive to movement. 'We are going to read three chapters today.' I'm pretty proud of my tone. Inflexible but not authoritarian.

She sighs loudly. 'Please never become a teacher.'

'Oi!' I flip open the text. I've never hated a book before. I'm morally against the idea, although it's true, I've never read *Mein Kampf*. For every book in existence someone has spilt part of themselves onto a page and then had the courage to hand it around. It seems disrespectful to hate it.

An hour later I come to the conclusion that at the very least I strongly dislike this book. I lay it down with a sigh of relief. 'I need another chocolate.'

'So do I.'

'I was the one reading.'

'I'm the one with the chocolates.'

We each have another, and then I reach for my bag. 'Guess what else I brought for after your nap?' I give a flourish worthy of a magician pulling out a rabbit.

Jasmine leans forward. 'What is it? I can't see.'

I bring the bottle closer. Her eyesight has not improved. 'Nail polish. I thought I could paint your nails.' I wait for her to look excited. 'Y'know. A bit of colour.'

She swallows. 'I can't have nail polish for surgery.'

'You're not going into surgery! You're not leaking, are you?' I don't give her a chance to reply. 'They said you could come home soon. There's no need to worry about surgery.'

She lays back against the raised bedhead, undecided. She looks tired. She looks nervous. I wait. I can't rush her. She has to make this decision for herself. Hospital-life is good at taking away decisions, great at removing risks, and even better at destroying hope.

'I have a cannula in my foot,' she says at last.

'Not in your toe nails.' I counter.

She grins. 'That's your polish, isn't it? I can tell. What's it called, *'Gothic Black'*?'

I whoop inside. 'It's grey!' I glare.

"*Depressing Dawn?*"

"*Charcoal*", actually.' I poke out my tongue. 'It's very dignified.'

'For a vampire.' She pushes her feet out from the hospital issue blanket. 'I thought you wanted to cheer me up, not depress me.'

'Do you want your nails painted or not?'

Chapter Thirteen: A Painful Routine

Brrrp. Brrrp. I roll over, eyes closed, and fumble for my alarm. *Brrrp. Brrrp. Brrrp. There.* Silence, beautiful silence.

I roll onto my back. If Mum is well I'll summarize my health-law lecture. Check the job-release sites. Write out practice interview questions, and the devotion for the next uni Bible study, and I'd really love to edit more of my novel... I slide out of bed and shrug on my purple dressing gown. Locating both my phone and the door in the caramel-coating of early morning, I leave my room.

Mum's talking. To whom? I pause at the top of the stairs and flick my phone. The screen lights up. 7.30 am. I've slept in. Her voice is coming from the bedroom next to mine, but it's too loud for her to be speaking to Dad. It can't be Aunty Berna because she hasn't slid into the slurred consonants of Dutch-English. She's using her Polite Voice.

I freeze. No. No. *No.* Jasmine's coming home tomorrow. She's all better. *She is.* Sticky with dread, I push open my parent's door. Mum turns to meet my eyes, corded phone to her ear. *Hospital,* she mouths. I freeze in the doorway.

There's a creak behind me. Dad's coming up the stairs. Mum must have beaten him to the second receiver before he could get to the downstairs landline. He nudges me into the room. I lurch forward, feeling his warmth on my back, and am reassured by the simple fact that he towers over my shoulders. We stand together in the middle of the room and wait.

'You poor thing. Did you sleep at all?' Mum's voice mellows, and I know she's now talking directly to Jasmine.

I jiggle. Dad is breathing hard and it's not from walking up the stairs. 'What'd they say?' His whisper in my ear rustles like the sad remains of a cobweb, the nightlong work of a spider, torn apart before the dew has even dried.

'I dunno.'

Mum meets our eyes, twisting the line from her insulin pump around her finger. *She's leaking,* she mouths. Leaking. The word of doom. I shuffle further in and drop onto the bed. The master bedroom is darker. If mine is caramel then theirs is navy-grey, soft shadows from the block-out curtains sitting heavily beside the queen bed and twin lamps. I can't look at anyone. Can't think too hard about what I've just heard. Not if I'm going to be of any use today. I close my eyes.

'What do you mean she's leaking?' I hear Dad explode.

'Shhh! I'm still talking to her!' Mum's voice hisses. Then a movement. I guess she's covering the mouthpiece. 'She's upset.'

So am I. *Bloody* upset.

At last Mum hangs up the phone. I swivel around, and take a handful of quilt in both hands. Squish it tightly. Open my eyes.

'That was the hospital.' Dad makes a 'go on' motion. 'She leaked through the night. They're fasting her. They're going to operate again.'

'Again?' Apparently.

'How?' Biology and human frailty.

'Why?' God only knows.

I don't cry. I gather my things and head to the car. I drive the hour and a half to the hospital, and I smash a hand against the steering wheel the entire time. I need to feel something, because every other part of my body is grey and heavy. Flipping my indicator, I turn down the street to the hospital and stop.

In the back of my mind I know I need to trawl up the road looking for two hour parking. I need to avoid university students and patients and pensioners. I need to slow down behind stopping busses and avoid the roadworks on the street with the overhanging bushes. A thought emerges out of the muzzy mess between my ears.

Someone from church gave us money for parking. We were going to save it for emergencies. Save it for Mum when she's not feeling well. I am numb. Lifeless. My body has decided not to work today. How considerate of it. How absolutely thoughtful. Couldn't have picked a better day myself. I park in the paid car-park beneath the hospital and switch off my *Moby Dick* audio book. Is this an emergency? I don't even care.

Clenched fists. Clenched jaw. Above all, clenched heart. It's just another operation. You'd think I'd be used to it by now. *Buck up Emily.* She was going to come home tomorrow. *Well now she's not, so get over it.* I arrive at the foyer of the Children's Hospital and I can't see a thing. It's as though someone has turned on a smoke machine. I know the nurses like to decorate for Christmas, but honestly this is too much. My throat spasms. I rush blindly to the women's toilets and push the door open. There's someone inside. For a moment I stare in confusion, unable to process this latest obstacle.

I make it to the bubbler screwed to the wall just outside before the tears come. Better to cry now than in front of Jasmine. I face the silver basin and drink. And drink. And drink. And pray no one else is thirsty. It's a long time until I can see again. Deep breaths. One, two. One, two. Are you done now, Emily? She'll be wondering where you are. Step away from the bubbler. You can do it.

I tighten my shoulders, and wipe my face one last time. Can that group of doctors tell I've been crying? How about that workman? That nurse? I yank my chin into the air. Just you try and pity me. *Just you try*. The flight of stairs above the café is both too long and too short. I smile as I climb. It's not a fool-proof trick, but I've learnt it's very hard to cry with despair while you're smiling.

Here we go. Jasmine's ward. Deep breaths. You're going to be positive, Emily. You're going to be strong. Above all, you're going to cheer her up. *Oh Lord, I can't do this*. 'Hey Jay!' I enter her room, the recycled smile on my face. 'How're you? They rang us about the operation...' No! Don't think about the operation. '...I'm going to keep you company. I brought a colouring book, the adult one.'

Jasmine is sitting up in bed, a tiny person whose light brown eyes are following my every move. Her cheeks are tattooed with tear tracks. I bend over and deposit my bags on a spare chair, taking the opportunity to blink hard. 'There's plenty we can do to make the time pass—'

'I… I don't want to go back to theatre.'

I'm not going to cry. Quick, something happy, something happy. Unicorns, chocolate, charcoal nail polish – Her chin trembles. That does it. I break. Her eyes fill. In the time it takes to pull a blue hospital-issue curtain closed *(to be changed NOVEMBER 2015 the tag reads)* and slip off a pair of boots, I'm sitting on her bed. We weep soundlessly. Hair moist. Noses gunky. Arms entwined.

For once, no one interrupts.

'I wasn't going to cry,' I say after a while, looking up at the stained ceiling. I breathe in the smell of cleaning products and disappointment and little sister.

She chokes. 'You failed.'

'Really? I hadn't noticed.' We can't stop giggling once we've started. We laugh and laugh. 'You need to blow your nose.'

'I'm not allowed, remember?'

'Well you need to do something, because you have a ginormous booger hanging out.'

She reaches up a finger.

'Eww!'

'It's stringy!'

'Get it away!' We shake the bed with our laughter. I could take on the world. You can only fear something for so long. Jasmine's CSF is leaking again. The worst has happened and now it's the aftermath and so we live on.

The car chortles into life. Instead of another repair job through the nose, they're going to bore a drain into Jasmine's skull. She fasted today for nothing. Again.

'We want to divert the spinal fluid,' I can still hear the doctor explaining. 'Give it a really good chance to heal. Of course this procedure carries more risks…'

Out of habit I hit my indicator and my audio book at the same time. *Moby Dick's* gravelly narrator fills the car. *"Oh! My friends, but this is man-killing! Yet this is life."* I reverse out of the car-park, wheels screeching on the smooth surface. *"…hardly is [one hardship overcome], when—"* I switch my headlights on. *"… away we sail to fight some other world, and go through young life's old routine again."*

I approach the front of the lecture hall during the five minute break. Best get this over and done with.

All I can think of is Jasmine. I haven't seen her since the fourth operation. Whose wonderful idea was it to invent 'compulsory tutorials' and 'mandatory assessments'? Obviously someone who doesn't spend all their free, and not so free, time at hospital with their sister. 'Excuse me?'

The lecturer, a short man I barely know, turns to face me. He shuffles the papers on his lectern. 'Hello—?'

'Hi, my name's Emily. My sister is in hospital at the moment. I know you said we have to stay to listen to all the speeches, but my group's already done our presentation, so I was wondering if I could leave to visit her?' I wait for him to say 'yes'. I'm only asking because it's the polite thing to do. I don't really care about his permission, because I don't really care about passing his subject. Today all my concern is pinned on a single person. I shuffle my feet as he shuffles his papers. Time *doesn't* shuffle but stretches on and on.

Finally he sighs. 'Someone else came to me yesterday and told me *their* sister is in hospital.' He squints at me, still shifting the assignments in front of him. 'I hope this isn't becoming a trend?'

I gape and pull myself up to look him dead in the face. All five foot three of me is stiff with shock and irritation. 'My sister had brain surgery yesterday.'

He turns back to his papers. *Shuffle.* Another sigh. 'Very well.' A pause. Is he realizing how heartless he sounds? 'Hope she gets well soon.'

I smile nicely, turn nicely, and nicely march up the theatre slope to the double doors. There's absolutely nothing nice about my thoughts.

It's like the Sahara outside and Papua New Guinea inside. I fiddle with the air-con as I wait in the traffic. Even the air coming through the vents is as thick as the aura of melted ice-cream. Is that possible? Do ice-creams have auras? Perhaps I've got heat stroke. I am so *over* driving to the hospital. Sweat rubs her greasy palms over my forehead and neck. My hair isn't long enough to tie up. I wish I was bald again.

The steering wheel is still hot and it's been 45 minutes since I left. I think I'm going to get a permanent burn mark on the bridge of my nose from my sunglasses. After speaking to the lecturer my motivation seems to have drifted away in the 34 degree heat. I don't even want to see Jasmine. I don't know what I want.

It's a good thing I've gone through the routine a billion times before. I enter the children's neurological ward and I can't for the life of me remember if I parked the car, let alone locked it. Yet if the travel is easy, the visiting isn't. I have to force myself to ring the doorbell. To my surprise I manage a smile at the nurse who lets me in. I don't even have to use my fingers to bend my lips into a curve.

I pause outside her door. It's not that I don't want to see her... but I *don't*. She'll be in pain, and I've had more in-pain-Jasmines lately than I ever thought I would. No, scrap that. I've had more *Jasmines* lately than I ever imagined. We talk about her, visit her, love her, plan for her, dream of her—

'Emily!' Mum spots me at the door. I manage another smile (I'm getting good at this!) and step inside.

There she is. The bed furthest away from the door. A white huddle. *Oh Lord, I can't—*

She looks up and meets my eyes. She smiles. Jasmine. My sister. At once everything else is superfluous. The hospital bed, the drips, the head bandage, the weird tube coming out from above her eyebrow... I don't see any of it. Just Jasmine.

I grin. 'I've missed you,' I say as I reach the bed, and it's true. 'So much.' The heat and the grumpy lecturer and the crowded roads wash away. I came to make Jasmine feel better, and instead it's me she's cheered up. Another normal, everyday paradox.

I sit beside her and for a single moment I am perfectly happy.

Chapter Fourteen: Seventeen Today!

I stare at the selection of cakes. These are The Sort We Don't Buy. The expensive sort. The sort that even though they are single servings look like miniature wedding creations, draped in chocolate swirls and gooey dulce de leche. 'That one please.'

The tall boy nods. He has a mop of blonde curls and a starched white uniform. I wonder if he's a student? I scored my first interview the other day, a radiography position at a hospital five hours from home.

'Takeaway?'

'Sorry, yes please.' He slides my choice carefully onto a piece of white cardboard, and eyes the bags slung around me. I feel sunburnt and suspect my face is shiny red. I left home at eight, and it took me thirty minutes to find street parking, then another fifteen to walk to the shops.

'Someone's birthday? For a friend?'

'Sister.' I smile. 'She's turning seventeen, but she's in the Children's, so I thought I'd bring her cake.'

He deftly folds the cardboard into a box, sliding the flaps together. 'You got the day off school?'

I lift both eyebrows. 'I finish uni in a few weeks. I'm job-hunting.'

He blinks. 'Oh.' Not even his mistake can squash my need to smile this morning. I grin as I duck to hunt for my wallet. Home-made caramel slice, home-made brownies, a happy birthday sign Mum insisted upon... there it is. He nods and hands me the change. 'Enjoy! Hope she has a lovely birthday.'

'Me too.'

'Happy birthday Jazzy-girl!' I peer around the curtains. Two nurses look up. They're bed-bathing her.

'Thank you.' Jay smiles widely. 'Guess what? They're going to clamp my external drain today so I can sit up!'

'Oh good!' I juggle boxes and bags. Having closed curtains reduces the floor space considerably. I back out. 'I'll hug you properly in a sec.' *When you're dressed.* I deposit all the food (minus the cake) in the patients' fridge and spend a few minutes scrawling forbidding labels and sticking them on all the plastic bags.

'Emily?' A familiar nurse. I know her name.... I do.. I glance at her name tag. *Sharon.* Knew it.

'Hello!' I can't stop smiling today.

'I wanted to catch you before you go back to Jasmine. Some of us are planning a surprise party for her in the common room this afternoon.' Her voice is a low murmur. 'We're trying to get permission to bring her in the wheelchair, but it depends how clamping her drain goes. Is anyone else coming that we should wait for?'

'Umm, yeah, Mum's coming this afternoon – she's hoping to feel better by then – and I think some of her school friends were going to drop in at some point... to surprise her too.'

'Okay, we'll time it around that and see how we go.' Sharon smiles, and it's big and genuine.

'Jas'll be thrilled. Thank you so much. She'll really love it...' I want to say more, but haven't got the words. Do they do this for all patients? It will make Jasmine's day. All of a sudden my slice of fancy cake seems rather small and silly, but it doesn't matter. Jay is going to have a wonderful time.

'Ooh, so pretty!' Jasmine is nothing if not an appreciative recipient. She clucks over the cake, cheeks flushed and eyes sparkling. Tiny strands of damp hair curl at her neck. 'Look at the chocolate swirl. Where did you get it?'

'A shop.' Nonchalant.

'How did you know it was there?'

Apparently that's the most important question. 'I've seen it before.'

'Are there a lot of cakes?'

'Heaps.' I gesture to show her exactly how many (a hospital room full). 'Do you like it?'

'Yes! I want to take a photo.'

'Then you need to taste it.' I search for leftover cutlery from breakfast. Jasmine waves me towards her bedside drawer and I pull out an unopened packet.

'You too.'

'It's your cake.' I make the token protest. We eat together.

'Fooff. I'm full.' Jasmine leans back.

'I should braid your hair.'

'No.' Her messy bun flops to one side.

'It's your birthday!'

'It hurts too much.' She brushes her fingertips over the tube projecting from her head. Her fringe is still purple from the pre-surgical iodine wash. 'It always feels like hair is pulling.'

'I'll be gentle.'

'Can't I just leave it like this?'

'How about clothes?' I try, thinking of all the visitors she'll be having. 'I brought a dress.'

'I like the gown. It's comfortable-er.'

I shrug. I've got several hours to convince her before her school friends arrive. 'So… what do you want to do?'

The morning streaks by like a released balloon. After lunch I can almost hear the wrinkled rubber bulb flop to the ground. I pick up the wrappers from the ice-cream I brought and head to the bin. 'I think it's time for a nap.'

She looks sideways at me. She's still not allowed to sit up. 'It's my birthday! Besides, I'm not tired.'

I raise my eyebrows. 'You will be.' All morning people have been in and out. The music therapists surprised her with a gift of noise-cancelling headphones. HAPPY BIRTHDAY was printed on her lunch form. A huge bouquet of cut-up fruit arrived from some family friends. We have enough flowers to start a small florist. And there's more to come.

'Just close your eyes.' I close my own. It's all too easy. 'Ahh.' I let myself sag into the chair. Or at least as much as one *can* sag on unforgiving plastic. Anyone would think these chairs held a grudge against humanity…

Jay giggles. 'What?' I open one eye. 'Shush! We're sleeping.' The giggling continues. 'Or at the very least, *I'm* sleeping.' I pretend to snore. Soon we're both giggling.

'Right!' I stand up. 'Apparently me being here is too distracting. I'm going for a walk. *You* are going to close your eyes and rest.' She giggles even harder at my ferocious glare. Mouth twitching, I escape.

In the common room I ring Mum. 'Hey, how are you?'

'How's Jasmine? I'm getting ready now. I'm well enough to drive at least.'

I read between the lines and frown. 'Don't rush. She's had a great day so far, and she's sleeping now. Everyone's been giving her presents and I bought her a slice of fancy cake. I figured she should have cake on her birthday.' Silence. 'Mum?'

'I was going to buy cake from Woolworths but you said not to because it wouldn't all get eaten...' I don't need to be able to hear her hurt, I can feel it. Deep in my stomach. Her illness has robbed her so many times of opportunities to show she cares, and now I've robbed her of one more.

'It's just a slice,' I rush. 'From a fancy shop that I've been to before. I wanted it to be a present from me...' And I didn't want you to complain about how much it cost. And I wanted to be the Provider of Cake. And... perhaps I've forgotten how to share.

By the time I return to the ward, Jasmine is fast asleep. I draw one curtain and flop back into the chair by her bed, unable to pack away my grin of triumph. Nap time for both of us I think.

'Emily?' I snap open my eyes. Mum's standing in the doorway, handbag over her shoulder, plastic bag handles looped around her wrist, snagging on her watchband.

'She's asleep.' I gesture at the bed.

'So were you,' she says.

'Not quite.' I give a deliberately sheepish smile so she won't worry. 'How was the drive?'

'Okay.' Mum puts down her bags. 'I parked beneath the hospital. Are the nurses really—'

'Shh!' I glance down. Jasmine's still asleep. *Apparently.* 'C'mon…'

We whisper in the corridor. 'I can't believe—'

'…and they brought a present too—'

'—do it for all the children?'

'Now you're here, we just need to wait for her to wake—'

'Hello Carla.' Another familiar nurse interrupts our Hospital-Appreciation-Party. 'As Emily may have told you…'

I wander back into Jasmine's room. She's awake.

'Where's Mum?' Jay glances at the handbag and plastic bags which weren't there when she closed her eyes.

'Talking to the nurse. You were out like a light. I knew you were tired!'

'Were you bored?' She looks concerned. I roll my eyes. That doesn't deserve an answer.

'Happy birthday, Jasmine!' Mum comes in, arms outstretched, huge smile. I wonder who's more excited. They meet in a hug on the bed. Something about Jasmine relaxes as I've noticed it only does when Mum or Dad are present.

I can wrap my quick-learnt maturity around myself tighter than spandex but it's no substitute for the real thing. Still, I'm pretty proud I was able to pre-empt Jay's need for a nap. After that success I can retire for the day, happy.

'Ready to go for a ride in the wheelchair?' Mum and Jasmine pull apart. The navy scrubbed nurse folds her arms and beams. You'd be mistaken for thinking she was offering us this week's winning lottery numbers.

For a second I see the familiar hesitation creep into Jasmine's mouth. She's worried she'll leak. She's worried she will get a migraine.

I don't blame her, but I flinch inside. What seventeen-year-old fears sitting up ninety degrees? I know the answer only too well. 'Okay!' Jay says. I see the exact moment hope wins out against worry; freed, her lips curve into a smile. I'm proud of her.

It's a feeling I'm still getting used to.

It takes the combined efforts of Mum, the nurse and me to convince Jasmine to at least put a grey vest on over her white gown. It's a testament to how little energy she has that she can't be bothered to change out of the one garment created solely to be easily taken off. This is the little girl who point blank refused to wear my hand-me-downs when we were children because they were 'ugly'. Never mind that they were already second-hand from my older cousins.

I wheel Jasmine out of her bedroom and strain my ears for noises sounding like party preparations. She is going to be so surprised. As we walk along Mum wears a look of secret anticipation and I know she's thinking the same thing.

'I'm out of bed!' Jasmine twists and turns, gazing over the wheelchair armrests into other patients' rooms as we pass. 'Whee!'

Don't ask where we're going. Don't ask. Down the hall we go, me pushing, Mum walking, Jay sitting and the nurse haranguing the drip pole. Wheels rattling, our peculiar procession arrives intact at the common room. Jay shifts. 'Why are we – oh!'

'Happy birthday to you! Happy birthday to you! Happy birthday dear Jas—'

I stop pushing with a jolt. *'A small party,'* the nurse had said. *'A few nurses. Some food.'*

Sausage rolls, party pies, chicken nuggets. Caramel slice, brownies, potato wedges. A huge blue and pink cake with a fondant bow and *'Happy 17th Birthday'*. No one in our family has *ever* had a cake like that. The usual common room odds-and-ends have vanished and the ceiling is draped with green and blue streamers. Tables I didn't know existed are arranged in a long row and covered with white cloth. Music is playing, I spy an ipod propped on a chair near the long windows. A small pile of wrapped presents sits at the head of the table.

'For me?' Jasmine squeaks.

She only lasts fifteen minutes in the end, the abrupt change in pressure giving her a massive migraine. The entire time she's paler than the white gown she's still wearing. The entire time she looks rather tiny and daunted: a baby-animal out of its native habitat. The entire time she's beaming like nothing in the world can possibly snatch away her happiness.

We take photos. Jay, Mum, me, her team of nurses and even the endocrine registrar, pager clipped to her belt. I wish I could capture on my phone the happiness of these people as they celebrate with Jasmine. Ten, twenty years older, all divided by profession and race and belief, all united as they joke and laugh and cheer her on. If goodwill were to manifest physically at this moment it would flood the entire room with a golden glow, and outshine even the spitting, effervescent sparklers on Jasmine's cake.

'SURPRISE!' The school-uniformed teenagers tumble into the hospital room, clutching flowers and wrapped presents and cake. A boy reels in a ginormous golden floating letter 'J'. The girl next to him giggles.

More friends than I expected. Is it 'cool' now, to visit someone in hospital? *Don't be cynical.* Just because she's popular… I lurk close by as Jasmine wavers between surprised tears and laughter. She goes with a bit of both. I haven't seen her so carefree since before her diagnosis.

'She had no idea you were coming,' I say, sensing a hesitation in the wave of young visitors as they begin to progress past the obligatory birthday greetings. 'You're lucky I convinced her to get dressed!' They burst into laughter and the ice rushes away in a flood of questions and exclamations.

'What does that do?'

'Guess what happened in biology!'

'Trish baked, but it sort of began to melt…'

'When I was at the balloon shop the man asked—'

I cross the room to get more seats and then beat a retreat. In the corner Mum is talking with the parent responsible for one of the carloads. Sympathetic nods and hushed questions seem to be making up the majority of the conversation. I shuffle so I'm inconspicuous at the back of the teen crowd. Far enough away to tune out the raucous laughter and sudden whoops, close enough that I can slip in at an awkward question or petering conversation.

Sitting up in bed, Jay is giggling uncontrollably. I relax. It's so *nice* not being responsible for keeping a smile on Jay's face. So *nice* not to have to guide the conversation or suggest the next diversion, as I do when it's just the two of us.

There's a lightness hanging off Jay's words which is new to me. These teenagers are achieving something I haven't managed in six weeks of visits. Should I be jealous? Mostly I just feel relieved. It's not my duty to oversee every facet of Jay's happiness. It doesn't matter that I so often fail in patience or resort to bossiness. It's not the end of the world that I didn't understand the importance of her pleas for dry shampoo until she cried in frustration. I don't need to beat myself up because some days I want to throw her melting cup of ice in her face instead of getting a fresh one.

I ponder my mixed motives for being the one to bring cake. Jay's happiness is not all up to me. I don't have to be her everything. I knew that theoretically, but today in hospital I know it practically. I learned to share toys in preschool, but today I have learned to share my sister.

By the time everyone leaves and Dad arrives after work, I'm even happier to take the back seat.

We've settled into the contented, post-celebration hum of reading cards and exclaiming over how nice everyone has been. I close my eyes and hang my legs over the plastic armrest. Imagine if this is it. If this really is the end of the journey, the happy ending we've all been waiting for. Jasmine back home in the currently predicted five days, and I back to being a student in her final weeks of university.

Nothing to worry about but the graduation ball. Nowhere to go but the beach. Just long days and a new friend to enjoy, instead of a live-in irritant to avoid. With the taste of cake in my mouth and the giant golden 'J' bobbing about the ceiling, I dare to believe this idyllic future is just around the corner.

REFLECTION
Moment by moment it comes

'I could never do that,' people say, when they hear stories of others living through tough times. 'I don't know how they did it.'

If there's one thing I've learnt, it's that you never live through 'that' or 'it' all in one go. You never experience the full force of tragedy in one hour or even one day. Instead you live through it piecemeal. First you experience the horror and shock of unwelcome news. Then you live through sharing it to others. Then you deal with the practicalities: the mundane minutiae of chores and applications and grocery shopping. Often you're caught up in this for days, weeks, months. Lastly you start to grieve what could have been and deal with the emotional aftershocks of a changed life.

Tragedy from a distance often seems insurmountable; tragedy close up can be boring and tedious. It's still awful of course, but when I look through my diary entries during Jasmine's hospitalisation, I find that there are good days and bad days. There are tiring days and exhausting days. There are brief flashes of joy and short stabs of terror. We learn of tragedy in an instant, but we live it out one day at a time. In doing so, we never, like C. S. Lewis once remarked, live through 'the thing itself'.

I'm not belittling tragedy. Instead, I'm embracing and welcoming the grace which comes with being mortal. All of life, the good and the bad, comes to us one hour, one minute, one second at a time. It arrives in bite-sized pieces, as though we were infants consuming a hated vegetable and a taste of dessert by turns. Sometimes it's a tiny taste, a mere lick of icing: a smile, an opportune car park, a well-brewed coffee. Other times our Father gives us an entire bite of cake, cherry included: a seventeenth birthday party, a surprise 21st. Each time the burst of sweetness reminds us that one day the vegetables will be finished and the entire dessert will be before us.

Take heart, friends. It's easy to imagine tragedy and extraordinarily difficult to picture grace big enough to help us bear it. Yet both exercises are futile. The first because tragedy never plays out as we expect, and the last because God does not give us hypothetical grace. Instead, he provides us with the strength to live through each minute as it comes; each minute and not a single one more.

Breathe in, friends. If you can't get through the week, know that you don't have to, not all at once. We live day by day. Some days we die a little and other days we are bountifully refreshed. **Moment follows moment with grace enough for each.**

PART THREE

Chapter Fifteen: It Matters to Me

'How long?' I ask the star-scattered sky. 'How much longer is this going to continue?' I lean against the cool red body of my car. The tyres are warm and rough against my calves. My stomach is full of hot, thick custard which rises with each passing second, like a lapping, tepid pool. I try and swallow it down.

The light outside the garage tosses genial yellow over the dark driveway, over my settling car, over me. I can't go into the house, not yet. We wrapped people up in toilet paper at youth group tonight. I ran around with the flapping mummies and laughed with the loudest of the teens. I did everything possible to forget.

I gulp big breaths of night time air. Perhaps if I get enough of the stuff inside me the sickly custard will retreat. I feel so ill. 'How long?' I whisper. If I go through the front door it will all become too real and I will cry again. *I want to run, Lord.* I want to take the selfish option. I don't want anything to do with pain or sadness anymore. It hurts too much.

Jasmine's spinal fluid is leaking again. Tomorrow they're going to insert a permanent internal shunt from her brain to her stomach in a fifth attempt to contain the fluid. Three days ago she was sitting up in bed and laughing as the cleaning lady, her shift finished, insisted on leading yet another chorus of 'happy birthday'. The memory feels like it's floated over from another lifetime. It's too full of hope to be part of my story.

I open my stinging eyes as wide as I can and tilt my head back, until my throat stretches. Why are there so few stars? Why are they so far apart? Tonight, it seems, even the sky doesn't have the energy to be beautiful.

I haven't had many words these past few days, so I've taken to stealing ones already written.

I have a new favourite poem, courtesy of a trip down Google's rabbit hole. The woman who wrote it has a name like something out of Harry Potter and it's already slipped my mind. Yet for some reason I can't get her words out of my head. They tumble around, mixed up and out of order.

My orders are to fight.

I reverse out of my driveway and battle the traffic, dreading what I will find when I reach the hospital.

'Can't move.' Jasmine pants. She's lying stretched out, neck at an odd angle, body fighting the alien tube inside her. 'Everything hurts.'

The back of my throat disappears. 'Oh, Jay.' I wish I could touch her. 'You poor thing.'

'Don't.' She growls. A long hand flaps. It's the only movement she can make without whimpering in pain. 'Don't say that.'

I'm at the hospital for eight hours that day, and each one of them I have to fight the urge to express sympathy. She doesn't want any more condolences. I understand. Neither do I.

Operation number five.

The servant craveth naught
Except to serve with might.
My orders are to fight.

'Hey! I'm home.' I close the front door, high on the *we-are-young-God-is-good-joy-fun-community* from my final university Bible study.

Dad meets me in the hallway. 'Jasmine is leaking again.'

'What?' I stare into his eyes and absorb his *old-too-sober-helpless-sad-exhausted-where-is-God*. I throw my joke award and small gifts down on the carpet. They're going to break open my little sister's head for the sixth time.

'When do they operate?'

Then if I bleed, or fail,
Or strongly win, what matters it?
My orders are to fight.

'Jasmine, you'll be pleased to know the operation went smoothly. We've adjusted your valve, mended the leak, and everything else seems to be in shape.' The surgeon rocks back on her feet. The Recovery suite is empty as usual. Mum, Dad and I stare at her from the other side of Jasmine's bed. We don't have the energy for much else.

The doctor could have said she'd replaced the shunt with an elephant's tail for all I care at the moment. I'm just grateful Jay has stopped whimpering. I don't know how much more pain I can watch. Is that incredibly selfish?

'Any questions?'

Jasmine blears up at the woman. Her mouth opens so slowly I wonder if she's actually going to say something or whether gravity will prove stronger than her facial muscles. 'I love you.'

If my snigger is slightly hysterical, well, I can't help it. It's the look on the surgeon's face. A hiccup comes from beside me. If I meet Dad's eyes I know I'll shatter into a fit of crying-laughter.

'Er… thank you Jasmine.' The surgeon replies. 'That's very… nice.'

I choke. Jasmine turns her head until she's looking at me. She frowns, a deep line of reproach spreading over her half-open eyes. 'I love her,' she says with stiff equanimity. 'She saved my life.'

Operation number six.

My orders are to fight;
God only doth prevail.
My orders are to fight.

I pick Mum up from her appointment and we wade home through the peak hour traffic. We reheat a meal someone from church has cooked and consume it in silence. An ache winds its weary way across my shoulders and down my arms. It's begun gnawing tunnels through my calf muscles when Mum's phone rings. I read the caller ID upside down. Dad.

'She's leaking?'
'Are you sure?'
'When?'
'The Neuro Team said it will be *tomorrow*?'
I let my elbows drop onto the table.
Operation number seven.

I was not told to win or lose,–
My orders are to fight.

I lie in bed and sleep hides in the distant corners of the night. Three operations in six days. How much longer must we fight? I don't know what winning looks like anymore, but I'm pretty sure this is losing. *My orders are to fight…if I bleed, or fail, or strongly win, what matters it?*

Oh Jesus, it matters to me. It matters so much.

36 kilometres away Jasmine is lying on her bed gazing up at the pock-marked ceiling. She hasn't been allowed to move from that position for the last seven days. I know that the smell of spinal fluid and Despair is running through her sinuses, because she tells me spinal fluid has a distinct scent and I know Despair does.

Jesus, she matters to *you*. I know this as certainly as I know where Jasmine is right now. Someone once told me that *'in the end our team always wins,'* because You always win. Win tonight.

Please.

Should I go?

I put my book down, and shift myself back on the window ledge. My shoulders press against the warm glass, and I imagine my scapulas sliding flat to soak up as much sunlight as possible. I twist my head so it's not resting on the window latch and close my eyes. I should go, shouldn't I?

The minister has called an emergency prayer meeting. He's even emailed around a fancy spread sheet so people can put their names in slots and shower Jasmine with prayer. I can't remember the last time our congregation has called an unplanned prayer meeting. Neither can my parents – and Mum's been attending this church since she was born.

My phone pings again. My Young Adults Whatsapp group is flashing with emoticons of praying hands and sad faces. We're not in this alone. It's really great. At least, Mum and Dad think so.

Should I go? I stretch out my legs to try and unnumb my backside. The window sill is neither broad nor particularly comfortable. It's a last resort. My final attempt to settle. I've begun timing myself on my phone, just so I actually stay in one room for longer than ten minutes.

I'm not used to being at home. I feel like a kid on detention, deprived of sensory input. I almost want to be at the hospital. Can visitors become institutionalised? Is that possible?

I give up, and leaving my book behind on the scarred floorboards, trail upstairs. My bedroom is pale blue; the pink one next door is empty. I belly flop onto my bed. I should go to the prayer meeting. Why am I even debating? Jasmine needs all the prayer she can get. I fumble for my phone and flick open my emails. I haven't actually read the church ones properly. Listening to my parents' reactions was enough.

'Good.' Dad croaked. 'They're praying.'

'How much everyone cares.' said Mum. 'Did you know Berna said the elder got teary in the pulpit when he announced Jasmine needs another operation?'

The email we sent fills the screen.

'Please pray for the surgeons. A new doctor is going to try a different procedure to stop the leak. They're calling a conference to discuss what is best. This operation is the last chance before they attempt open brain surgery which carries a very big risk.'

I scroll down, glancing at the long lists of names and times. So. Much. Prayer. Guilt squirms in my chest. I push myself down on the mattress. If only I could fall asleep. That would give me a brilliant reason not to attend. I catch that thought and wrangle it. No one's expecting me to be at the prayer meeting. I still feel uncomfortable though. Not about not going, so much as not *wanting* to go. When was the last time I prayed for Jasmine? Properly *prayed*, not just a whispered plea or a silent demand? I don't remember.

The guilt latches onto my shoulder blades, stripping away the warmth from the window pane. *I can't pray.* I know that's not true. I just don't want to. I'd rather do anything but pray. My thoughts are too tired, too hopeless, too beaten down by weeks of operations to fly anywhere near heaven. I close my eyes against the tears. *The operation's tomorrow, Lord. Will my prayer really make a difference?*

Being at the hospital feels like an accomplishment. Writing a new scene for my novel feels like a success. Prayer feels like a colossal waste of time. *You'll heal her if you want, and you'll let her die if you want, Lord. You already know what I want. I don't have the energy to ask for it. Oh Jesus. I long to please you. But I can't pray.*

I open my eyes and find the clock. The prayer meeting has started. Guilt turns to failure, crushing me back to the bed. Here I sit at home while others pray fervently for the healing of my little sister.

I wonder if it feels odd for them to be at the church building in the middle of the week. Perhaps this will be the first of many emergency prayer meetings. Not just for Jasmine, but for other people, locked in other tragedies. At least they are able to imitate you, Lord. At least someone can.

I suck in a breath. Could it be – I scrabble through the ramifications of my thought. At the moment I can't tell how Christ is being glorified in me… but when other people pray for Jasmine, they are imitating Christ's love. These people, busy with their own lives and trials and fears, are pouring out their energy and love onto me and my family. If Jasmine wasn't in hospital, they wouldn't have been given this same chance.

Oh Lord, can it be true? I need this hope, this promise that you are being honoured, that something good really is winking into being even in the midst of despair. It is true, isn't it? Through the suffering of this seventh operation other people are loving in beautiful ways.

I relax. My bed feels warm and cosy, as if I've brought the sun inside with me and tucked it beneath my quilt. Was it like that before? I don't remember… I close my eyes again, but this time it's prompted by assurance, not guilt. There are people who love Jasmine praying. They've got the energy and the passion I lack. They are ensuring that this tragedy is not wasted.

I breathe out. I could go to sleep now. Actually, I rather think I will.

Chapter Sixteen: When Surviving is Dangerous

'You can come in.'

Mum, Dad and I follow the doctor into Recovery. It's late in the day and the nurses' station is a-babble with handovers and farewells. All the beds in the U-shaped room are empty save two. One holds my sister.

'It was successful?'

The doctor stops before we reach the bedside. 'Yes, it went well. We patched the leak up nicely.' I'm afraid his words don't relieve me. After all, that's what he said last time, and the time before that, and before that, and... here we are again: operation number seven.

We crowd the bed. 'Jasmine?' The white huddle shifts. Betadine-stained skin gives birth to translucent coils in all directions. One stretches out from her side and has a drip stand all of its own. That's new. 'How are you feeling?'

'Mum?' Jay gives the impression of someone turning their head, without actually achieving the action. This is more than she's been able to do the other times, in fact, she seems quite lucid. Perhaps there really is something special about the number seven?

'Hello Jasmine,' the surgeon draws up a plastic chair and sits so he's eye level with the bed rails. 'I'm Frank, one of your doctors.'

'Frank?' She peers through messy hair. The bandage strapped across her face is twisted under her nose like a broad white moustache. 'Frank… Frankenstein. I'm going to call you Frankenstein!' She announces with all the aplomb of Queen Elizabeth at a knighting ceremony.

'Jasmine!' Mum and Dad stare. I try hard not to giggle. I take back my earlier assessment. I won't be choosing number seven anytime soon. Normally Jasmine is good at jokes, but bad with strangers. This is not normal Jasmine at all.

'The surgery went really well.' Frank-not-Frankenstein continues with admirable calm. 'We patched up your nose again.'

'My nose!' It's said in a trembling crescendo; the sound of sheer terror. She begins to cry. We do our best not to look bewildered.

'Shh, it's okay. You had a leak, remember.' Frank is stoicism personified. 'We operated to fix it.'

'Oh.' The tears stop.

In the silence we can hear the adults huddled around the bed next door. *'After this we'll drop by McDonald's and get you …'*

Jay stiffens. 'I want McDonald's!'

'What?'

'You don't even like McDonald's,' Mum protests.

'Oh.' Her body relaxes for a second. Then, 'I want McDonald's!'

This is beginning to get embarrassing.

'Jasmine,' Dr Frank interrupts, 'I need to tell you about the bandage around your nose. It has to stay there for three days—'

'Three days?' She latches onto these new words with the tenacity of a sheepdog and lifts an arm slowly into the air. Lying on her back, dressed all in white, she looks like a spectre rising from beyond the grave. 'Jesus was in the tomb for three days!'

I burst out laughing.

'Jasmine!' Unflappable Frank is flapped. He brings his voice back down with, I suspect, great effort. *'Please* try and concentrate. I need to tell you about your nose…' He runs through his post-op instructions. I wonder if it's home time for him after this. Either way, I'm sure he's dying to get away.

Jasmine asks to kiss him. He politely declines. She appears heart-broken. He continues his instructions. Jasmine embraces her inner Pollyanna and becomes very happy with the world in general.

'Now,' Frank finishes, 'You've been very brave so far and—'

'I know!' she interrupts, but before I can laugh at the twin look of amazement on Mum and Dad's faces, she bursts into tears. 'Oh no!' she wails, loud enough that everyone flinches. 'I've got a big head!' She turns to Mum. 'Do I have a big head now?'

Dr. Frank makes his escape and I dissolve.

'You've been here since the morning and it's 9 pm.'

'I know. But I'm young,' I glance at Dad, 'and healthy,' I look at Mum. 'You know she'll want someone to stay until she moves back to the ward.'

'You'll have to drive home in the dark.'

'I want to stay,' I say, and if my determination is counterfeit, well, at least it's of superior quality. Perhaps bravado, too, lies in the domain of the young.

They hug me, and do the standard hover-hug over Jasmine who's fallen asleep again. 'Don't make it too late.'

'I won't.' I'll be as late as I need to. Recovery is empty now. Beds stand in rows like gravestones. Painted seagulls crawl across the plaster walls and a lighthouse glares blindly beneath a neon exit sign. Three nurses pack up the darkened admin station, their footsteps echoing across the vacant space.

I sit and weave my hand through the bed rails. Jay moans. I unglue the melting ice-block from its Styrofoam cup and push it through the bars. It slips sideways on her closed lips. Eyes shut, she sucks greedily. The white paper wrapper turns transparent and stickiness drips down my fingers. I close my own eyes and try to remember how far away I parked.

A whimper. 'Jay?' My several-decibels-below-a-whisper voice is excellent. 'What's wrong?'

'Marghgh.'

'The surgery went really well.' *You didn't die.* 'Mum and Dad have gone home but they'll be back in the morning.'

Silence. She's asleep again. Drip. Drip. Drip goes the ubiquitous lemonade ice-block. It's practically a rite of passage in hospital, and as such I think they should be offered to family as well. It's so hot in here. My hand aches, and I remember I'm still holding the Rite of Passage between the rails. I jiggle, coating Jay's lips in liquid sugar.

She screams. I smash the ice-block against the metal bars. 'Jay! Are you—' Her next scream is deeper, longer, the voice of unendurable agony. I leap to my feet. The three nurses rush over.

'Where's the pain? Jasmine? Talk to us. You need to—'

'Hereeee.' She clutches at her stomach.

Confusion. They operated on her nose. That's what the notes say. Did the surgeon leave instructions? A whispered consult ensues beneath three bent heads. *She's not deaf, you know.*

'What is it?' I hold Jay's hand through the bars. She pants, tongue seizing rhythmically, struggling to eject agony. It's as though someone flicked a switch, launching her straight from muzzy semi-consciousness to wide-awake pain.

'She's full of urine,' one nurse says, breaking from their little bevy. 'That's what's causing the pain. Jasmine dear, I'm just going to feel your stomach.' Jay screams. I twitch, and manage to stop myself from ripping away the nurse's prodding hand. Jay's stomach is as taut as a beach ball and just as big.

'Perhaps there's some sort of blockage. We'll give it a few minutes. I need to consult her notes, see when her last dose of antidiuretic was.' She pats Jasmine on the shoulder. 'Hang on there, dear. Try to relax.'

'Where are they going?' Panic blazes in her eyes. 'It hurts!'

'I know,' I soothe. 'They're just going to check the notes.'

'Help!' She screams, flailing from side to side. 'Help!'

'Jasmine! Deep breaths.'

She shudders. I reach out to pat her. 'Don't touch me!' Her fist just misses my forehead. 'It hurrtttsss!'

I can't watch this. I can't. 'It's going to be okay.'

She seizes, as if struck by a shot of pure torment. 'Ah, ah, ah!' I've never seen a woman in childbirth and I never want to. 'Take it away! It hurts!'

'I can't, I'm sorry, Jay. I'm so sorry.' I dare not touch her. I'm engulfed by helplessness, and I can feel it lapping against my earlobes, threatening to pull me under. I press my drowning body against the bed rails and talk. She screams. On and on we go, each of us trying our hardest to block the other out.

Ping. I scrabble for my phone. Mum.

Have you left yet?
Why not?
Leave now
You must be tired

I haven't left because your daughter is hysterical and I can't even touch her without provoking a wild murder attempt, so my exhaustion really isn't the primary feature of concern. How to say that in 160 characters? I hold the bed bars and type with one thumb.

Will leave soon. Jasmine's woken up now. Shouldn't be long.

Sleep well.

A minute later a text alert interrupts a particularly long scream.

You too. Don't make it late.
We've left the light on.

It's a while before my eyes are clear enough to see the on-screen keyboard.

Thanks. I type.
Love you.

A nurse approaches, short brown hair clipped back from her ears. I recognise her as one of the original triumvirate. 'We're going to get a portable ultrasound, see how much fluid she's got in there.'

Wee. Why not just say it? She's full of wee. I smile my thanks. 'There's nothing you can give her in the meantime? She's in a lot of pain.'

The nurse looks down at the bed with a wince. 'Sorry, no. Technically the anaesthetic should still be dulling most of her discomfort.'

Discomfort? I don't see Discomfort. The Agony right in front of me must be impeding my vision. Jasmine whimpers. Is she attempting to keep quiet or is she too tired to scream? The nurse leaves. I can feel my sanity edging backwards, trying to snatch a lift. If only I could hold Jay's hand without her flinching!

'Arghgh!' Jay bucks against the sheets and thrashes her head. Tears splatter onto the pillow. I say nothing. I don't know if it's the right thing to say.

'I want to die.' She moans and her fingers find the bed rail. Her nails are bloodless. 'I want to die!'

'No you don't!' I strike away my tears, unable to believe that only a couple of hours ago she was calling Doctor Frank 'Frankenstein' and asking for McDonald's. 'You're just in pain! It's not going to last forever. I *promise* Jay.' My fury subsides. 'It's not going to be forever.'

I'm not lying. It's not exactly, objectively, *forever*. Still, it feels pretty close by the time a catheter is able to bring her pain down to a more manageable level. In novels people wonder how long they've been holding their breath; I don't even remember what normal breathing is.

I ghost through the corridors. They're too wide and too long. In fact, there's nothing right about them at all. They're people-less.

I reach the stairs and a living breathing human pops into being. He hurries up, I charge down. I see a medical registrar, called up to the wards. What does he see? A girl with hollow eyes and trembling mouth, pressing her laptop to her chest as if it's the only solid object left in the world? If this is what he sees, it does not surprise him.

I clack loudly across the plastic floor of the closed-up cafe. The wall clock ticks over to 10:30 pm. It's nice to be alone. Nice to be away from the screams.

Outside the cold inky air tousles my too-short hair. It rushes up and down my arms, and cocoons the black-red-yellow-white urban mosaic in particles of mystery. I like solitude, I remember. I like it very much. I open up to the night and let it push away the ravaging echoes of anguish and fill the crater of my inadequacy. For a few minutes its timeless waves slap against the edges of my chasm and disaster feels precious and pain seems beautiful.

The side street is dry and lightless. The shadows are substantial enough to hold at least two stalling black vans, let alone the deviants to drive them. I may never be seen again. A heady thrill of fear. I feel brave and good. I'm a knight errant charging off to battle. I'm a Romantic poet contemplating words of genius. This has been the worst night of my life and I have survived, and because of that it has become the best night. Nothing can stop me now.

Then I remember my parents and picture what they would say if I disappeared. The thought sends a cold wave rushing across my shoulders, melting my delusions. I quicken my pace, and begin looking over my shoulder.

Does gazing on someone else's agony always result in such false courage? Does it always give birth to this counterfeit euphoria? I shiver. I need to watch myself. Suffering vicariously is a dangerous thing. I almost began to believe that tragedy is glamorous, and by extension so am I.

    I click the locks and lean back in my car seat. Tonight I watched pain eat through a person like fire consumes a tree. I have looked on the hollow, crumbling remains and breathed in the acrid smoke. I have done my best to remember that Spring always comes, and that this is not the end. But that doesn't make me a hero. Just tired. I plug in my phone and start the ignition. As I drive away, leaving Jay to scrape together what Pain has left her, I know she is not alone. The One who has nurtured and cared for her all these years is doing so still. Pain burns and scars, but God can bring forth green shoots from even the blackest stump.

Chapter Seventeen: The Blessing of Being Seen

It's raining, it's pouring, and this time it's my own nose that's leaking...

It would probably be snoring as well, except unfortunately I'm awake. Rain patters onto the verandah roof, each drop splitting into a thousand as it lands on the corrugated plastic. I rub my eyes.

It was only a matter of time. Life has been crazy lately, I'm probably run down. No, scrap that. I *am* run down. It's to be expected when you're prepping for interviews, studying for final exams, and have a sister in a hospital ninety minutes away. I blow my nose for the twelfth time. A throbbing starts behind my eyes and I wince. I can't be sick. I stare at the water streaming down my window. I have so much to do.

Moist tissues congeal in my hand. Shrivelled tongue. Stewed mucous. I choke on the contents of my nostrils. I would give anything to be able to smell, even if it's just the stale tannin from my *midnight-can't-sleep* teacup on the bedside table. I shuffle towards my dressing gown. However awful I feel, Jasmine is bound to be feeling worse.

Fwwish woosh. Fwwish woosh.

My windscreen wipers are giving me a headache. Or did I have one before I was forced to flip them up to full speed? I can't remember. I've been circling the clogged streets for fifty minutes trying to find a park. That's the problem with visiting a hospital in a deluge. Not only is everyone driving at a *third* of their normal speed, but the Find-The-Closest-Parking-Spot Game has been turned up to Level: Deadly.

I manage to miss flattening a snowy-haired lady with her shopping bags (is she insane?) and a man in a suit (black umbrellas ought to have mandatory fluorescent patches), and ease into a curbside park. I wait. Is it my imagination, or is the rain lessening?

Definitely my imagination. I heft my bags out the door in front of me and step into a puddle. The whole street is one Olympic swimming pool, gutters overflowing around deserted signs which warn of *Road Work in Progress*. Yes, and pigs fly.

I put up my umbrella, untangle it from the tree branch above my head, and squelch my way to the hospital.

'Hey! It's a flood out there!' I stomp into the room and hunt for a suitable umbrella corner. Water whooshes out of my boots as if I'm wearing sponges. My socks cling tightly to my feet, rubbing in all the wrong places. Beneath my coat and jumper and shirt droplets of sweat slide like cold coins.

'Hey.' Jasmine rolls over.

'How are you?' I give up and dump the umbrella in the nearest niche, stripping off my scarf. Which pocket did I put my tissues in?

'Okay.'

'I have a cold.' I find them, damp and musty like they've been through the wash. I blow. 'I need a drink.' The thought of instant coffee makes my tongue curl. Thank goodness for complimentary tea bags. 'It took ages to park.' I can't manage a sentence longer than six words today, and don't even want to look at a syllable. My throat aches.

'You shouldn't have come.'

I eye her sharply. 'Are you okay?'

She shrugs. 'If you're sick you shouldn't have come.'

'I'm not sick.' Quick, retreat. 'Not *sick* sick. Just a cold. Besides, aren't you glad to see me?'

A small smile comes to her face. 'Yeah.' she whispers. She shifts against the bed sheets. She's never comfortable anymore, but there is something else happening. Something I'm missing. I frown. *Don't let her be sick, Lord.*

I kick a plastic chair to the bed and sit down. Tea can wait. 'Guess what?'

Is that a quarter of a fragment of interest in her eyes? I'll take it. She rolls her head towards me. 'What?'

Um… something huge. Something impressive. Something more exciting than parking and the state of the traffic and job interviews I didn't get and… *Got it.*

'Did you know…' I draw my voice out like a drum roll. 'You haven't leaked spinal fluid for…' I hold the tension and do frantic mental calculations. '… eight days?' My smile is genuine. 'That's a record!'

She grins, but it disappears too soon. I understand. How many times have we unwittingly rejoiced on the eve of an operation? Far, far too many.

'Everyone's praying,' I remind her. 'Have you had a wash?'

She shakes her head. I squish my lips together. At the moment Jay's worse company than my fellow drivers in the Find-The-Closest-Car-Park Game, but that is going to change.

Even if I have to drink the hospital dry of tea to do so.

I tease the long, betadine-stained strands apart. One thatch at a time. 'You're going to look so beautiful!' I hear something which sounds like a snort, but with my sinuses blocked and the shower-head running, it's a bit hard to tell. 'Doesn't it feel good to be sitting up? To have a proper shower?'

The head beneath my hands nods, but I don't hear anything I can construe into speech. She's tiring fast. So am I. Time to up my game.

'Ow! Stop!'

'Oh. Sorry!' I've pulled at a scar again. There's so many of them it's like avoiding a camel in a haystack. 'I promise it will look good when it's done.'

And it does. By the time she's back in bed her hair is tangle-free and I'm only a little wetter than when I first arrived. 'We should send a picture to Mum! First hair wash in three weeks! First time sitting up since the operation! We need to celebrate!'

Jay grins. It's amazing what a shower can do. 'I'll take it,' she says, fumbling for her phone. 'I've gotten good at selfies.'

'I'll believe *that* when I see it.'

When I return from making another styrofoam cup of tea (why are they so small? Is there a secret plot afoot to passively limit caffeine intake?), Jasmine's nurse is standing at the foot of the bed.

'Ah, there you are!' she says in her sharp Irish accent. 'I was just explaining to Jas that if you're happy to drive, she can go for a bit of a ride in the chair.'

'Ooh!' An idea springs up. Not sure where from. Certainly not my cotton-wool head. 'Can we leave the ward?'

Jasmine stares. It's been six weeks. The nurse nods. 'Don't see why not. As long as it's not for more than half an hour. Go grab a hot chocolate or something.'

We turn to the bed in anticipation. Jasmine looks like she's been offered a Christmas present and she's not sure if it's really for her. 'Really? What if I… leak?'

'It's been eight days,' the nurse reminds. 'If you were going to leak you would have done so already.'

'C'mon,' I whoop. 'Let's go!'

'Wheee!'

'Ow! Slow down!' Jay grips the hand rails. 'Everything's bumping.'

I paste an incredulous look on my face which she can't see. 'I'm walking at a normal speed.'

'I'm going to get sea-sick!'

'Wheelchair sick?' We laugh, but Jasmine's still has an uncertain edge. I push her into the lift as it opens. We squeeze in beside two doctors and a woman with a little boy. Jay meets my eyes. I nod firmly, and we both copy the remarkably bland expressions on the faces of our companions, as if we go up and down in the lift every day.

I hope she's whooping inside. I know I am. First time out of the ward for something other than an operation! I feel like someone should present us with a plaque in honour of the occasion. Halfway down the corridor the head in front of me lolls to one side. 'Jay? What is it?'

'Tired.' Floats back to me. 'My neck hurts.'

I relax my grip on the handlebars. Then I push off.

'Ooooh! Stop! Stop! You're too speedy!'

I laugh and don't listen until her complaints turn to whimpers. 'My head hurts.' she moans.

'I just wanted us to get there quickly,' I say. 'See. Here we are!' The corridor spills out into a cafe. I weave through the crowds and park her at a table. 'Wait here.' Jay rolls her eyes. I snigger and lock the brakes on the wheelchair.

Huge glass doors flood the place with natural light. Outside taxis crouch in the rain and patients connected to drips smoke cigarettes under the eaves. Yet inside, if I ignore the pager-laden woman in front of me and the two men in pale blue scrubs near the drinks fridge, I could be in any Sydney cafe.

'Two iced chocolates please.' My eye snags on the sweet display, '...and the caramel slice.' I wait without taking my eyes off Jasmine. She's hard to miss, a tiny slumped figure in a white gown at the far table.

'Surprise!' I dump the drinks on the laminate and let the paper bagged slice slide from my grip. 'We're celebrating!'

Her eyes light up. 'Wow!' The drinks are all swirled cream and chocolate power. Pretty impressive.

'I've got caramel slice too. How amazing does it look?'

'Yummm.'

I sip my drink and watch her energy wane. If she's this exhausted after twenty minutes out of bed, what's it going to be like when she's discharged in a few days?

Discharged. I bite into my half of the slice with gusto. We're so close. Once I get a job, this cafe visit will be the first of many. The icy milk is balm to my sore throat. I stretch out my legs and wiggle my toes. I could sit here for a long time. Jasmine's quiet but it doesn't matter. We have the whole afternoon ahead of us.

'Can we go back now?'

I put down my drink. Condensation leaks onto the table. 'Already?'

'I'm tired.'

'You don't want to stay a little longer? We still have time.'

She shakes her head. 'Please.'

'Okay. Do you want any more of your drink?' A minute gesture: no. I sweep our rubbish into a pile and locate a bin. 'One sec...' I bend to unlock the brakes.

'Already done.'

'Can you hold my drink?' I rest it in her lap. I've been savouring it too much and it's still half full. Her grip is unenthusiastic. 'Okay, off we go! We're off to see the wizard, the wonderful wizard of—'

'Hi dearies!' A grey haired lady snags us before we reach the lifts. Behind her is a folding table, its red-and-green cloth strewn with trinkets and baubles. 'How are you?'

'A bit tired,' I answer for us both, and continue to nudge the wheelchair forward with my knees. Another old lady smiles from behind the table. It must be some sort of pop-up volunteer gift stall.

'Here, take this.' The first lady smiles and holds out two crocheted stockings about an inch and a half high. 'One for each of you. A gift from us.'

'Are you sure?' The pocket-sized Christmas decorations are clearly part of their merchandise. They've even got tiny price tags attached, written in elegant old-school writing with crossed sevens and tailed ones.

'Please,' she encourages. Her companion smiles and nods.

'Thank you very much.' Jasmine says. The faces of the old ladies soften.

'Yes, thank you. Thank you very much. It's lovely.' I loop mine over my thumb.

'Get well soon!' They call.

I wait until we're a sufficient distance away. 'How nice!'

'They just gave them to us for free!'

I have my suspicions why. 'How old do you think they thought we were?'

'Hmm.' Jasmine's eyes begin to close just as the lift doors open. 'Young.'

In her hospital gown Jay looks about twelve. A really cute twelve (and yes, that's an objective fact). I wouldn't be surprised if when they start to put up Christmas decorations here they recruit her for the part of an angel. Her hair also looks beautiful, if I may say so myself. Which I can, I spent long enough on it. As people keep mistaking me for the younger sister, I'm under no illusion the ladies thought I was twenty-one. A little girl, pushing another little girl in a wheelchair, at Christmas: Prime pity material. Still…

I rub my forefinger against the tight woollen stitches as we wait for the lift to ding. It was nice of them to give me one when it is obvious Jay is the patient. My first Christmas present.

We re-enter the ward. Beneath the chattering, beeping veneer the rain thunders. I'm exhausted. I finish my drink as Jasmine lies silently on her bed, eyes shut. It's happening again. I meant to give her a celebration, and instead I've been given a gift myself. I don't even know their names, those two women. I'm sure they've forgotten about us already, and yet... I feel lighter.

The sort of lighter I feel on the rare occasion someone places their hands on my shoulders and says, 'now we've talked about Jasmine, how are *you* going?' The sort of lighter when a doctor stops to ask if I'm studying or working instead of using me as a portable telegraph machine or assuming I'm a fixture of the furniture.

Jasmine deserves the attention of course. She's the one who's survived seven operations. Still, it's nice when I get to share it. I realise that perhaps I've muddled up cause and effect. The women didn't give us gifts because we were 'cute'. They thought we were 'cute' and gave us gifts because first they opened their eyes and saw us. Not our labels, not our roles, but *us*.

The rain's cacophony softens into an almost lyrical sound. The ward suddenly feels cosy and safe, a warm, bright hub protected from the inclement weather. I shift so my legs are resting on the edge of an empty chair. I should plan which English text we're going to study this afternoon. Instead I look around at the plain white room with its bedraggled flowers and sleeping girl. I love her so much.

There are worse places to be on a rainy day.

'Look!' Jasmine giggles. I crane my neck. You wouldn't believe how amusing it is to watch people scurry through the rain from three storeys above. Jasmine's English text lies forgotten on the bed.

I blink. 'What is *that?* A rain jacket?'

She bursts into sudden laughter. The nap has done her good. 'It's a picnic rug!'

We snigger as two women sprint across the pavement clutching a green and yellow picnic rug over their heads. I pat around for another tissue. My nose won't stop leaking, but that's more than okay. *Jasmine's* hasn't leaked for eight days. There are definitely worse places to be.

Standing under a picnic rug in a downpour would be one of them.

All too much

DIARY EXCERPT
November 8, 2015 (55 days in hospital)

Found out this morning Jasmine is leaking again. It tested positive to Cerebral Spinal Fluid. That could mean open brain surgery. I'm still sick. And so, so tired. Of everything.

...I'd say I can't go on, except that's a bit melodramatic, and also a bit pointless. After all, I can. I have to. Because life doesn't conveniently stop when you feel like it ought... So what can I say? I was mentally preparing a Facebook post for when Jasmine came home from hospital - it was meant to be this week. Well. I think I'll say it here instead: God is good. Not because all that's happened to Jasmine has been good. It has not. But because that is His character.

...I'd hoped to reaffirm that knowledge with Jasmine by my side, at home, healed. Instead she's still in hospital, eight weeks and seven surgeries later. And that hurts. It's sad and horrible and helpless.

… I don't know what's going to happen. I don't know how many more times it's all going to just be too much. But one thing I do know: God is good. [For those who love him] 'all things work for good' [Romans 8:28]. I've never liked that verse, but I do now.

There's nothing else.

Chapter Eighteen: Give Me a Softer World

I wait until she's sitting at the dining table with a crossword. 'I got another interview.'

Mum puts the ragged piece of newspaper down. 'Congratulations. Where?'

I name a hospital past the Blue Mountains.

'That's far.'

'Not as far as Dubbo.' That was the location of my first interview. 'And I can choose to do a phone interview again.' I fiddle with an old Woolworths brochure. 'It's hard when we don't know what's going to happen with Jay.' People can get brain damage from open brain surgery.

Mum nods. Then she looks back down at her crossword. If only decisions were as simple as filling in black and white boxes: 'Tugs' is the answer to 3-down, not 'pull'.

'You always wanted to go rural,' she reminds me.

'I know. I still do.' I stare over her shoulder into the kitchen swamped with tentative afternoon sun. I wait for her to give me her opinion. This is Mum. She has a strong view on everything, from the correct way to hang washing, to whether eight-year-old me ought to pursue a career in coaster decorating ('that's not a proper job'). I wait some more.

Now I think about it, she's been giving her opinion less and less over the past few years. She said nothing five months ago when I told her I was going to shave my head. When I asked, her reply was: 'It's your head, not mine.' Is this going to be a similar occasion? 'It's your career, not mine'?

'What's a six-letter word which means 'to change direction'?'

Looks like it. I stand up. She's right. This is a decision I have to make alone. I'll be the one living out the consequences. 'Um, pivot? ... pivots? I don't know. Mum, I'm going to have a shower.'

'That's the wrong tense…' She fills a few boxes on the grey paper. '…Okay.'

Showers are brilliant places for thinking.

It's as if the enclosed space compresses and concentrates my thoughts so they become too heavy to drift away. I can even make fog-diagrams with a finger, though I have to remember to scribble them out afterwards. Too often I've come to shower, only to watch someone else's smiley faces appearing one by one on the smoggy glass as the steam builds. I don't have to worry about that today. That Someone hasn't had a shower here for over seven weeks.

I turn the hot tap and wait just out of reach. 'Right Emily.' I say. 'You're going to reach a decision by the end of your shower. You don't have enough energy to drag it on.'

Showers are also brilliant places for talking aloud. My voice is drowned out by the water pressure, diluting self-consciousness, maintaining privacy. I test the water temperature with my leg and twist the cold tap. It stabilizes into a warm flow and I move beneath the gushing head. *Mmm.*

'The thing is,' I tell the cloudy screen, 'I've always wanted to go rural. Half of my uni placements have been rural. This is my chance. Besides, there are more jobs rural. If I go rural I can work in a hospital. The competition's too high in the city hospitals, besides, I hated my placement there. There's always private practices, but they can be small and boring and political… I *really* don't want to work at one.'

I imagine a jury of little steam-people in front of me, nodding at my words. *Yes,* they murmur, *succinct presentation of all the facts. It sounds like you should go rural.*

'But now, Jasmine is sick.' I write 'rural' on the fogged plastic and then cross it out. I draw an arrow and write 'Jay'. 'She's in hospital and I don't know when she's going to come out. I don't even know what she'll be *like* when she comes out. It's been so long already. Besides, what will she need? What sort of care, what sort of support? If I'm living in *Whoop-Whoop* I can't help her or Mum or Dad.'

The little jury people nod in sync. *Yes, yes. That makes sense. You need to stay around to be here for her. That's the logical decision.*

'I know!' I spit shower water at the screen. I slash my hand across the words. 'It's the well-reasoned, realistic, logical decision, but I don't like it!' I breathe in. Control, Emily. If it's the right decision, which it is, there's no reason to feel awful about it.

'In an ideal world I would leave Sydney and live and work in a rural community.' I reason. I even sound convincing. 'But this is not an ideal world, so I have to stay. There's nothing wrong with that.'

I close my eyes. Nothing, except that I want that ideal world more than anything. Nothing, except that even if this decision is right, it still feels like a rogue dinosaur has come smashing through not only my future but also my identity.

Jasmine would stay near home and look after Mum. I would live rurally and overseas. Jasmine would have the grandkids parents always dream of. I would serve a community somewhere in desperate need. Jasmine would look after our parents in their old age. I would pop in and out and bring them tales of the world and my adventures.

It was the hinted, embraced, but unspoken agreement between us. 'You can be the eccentric Aunt Em,' Jasmine would say, 'and I'll cook meals and put them in those little plastic containers and my husband can drop them off at your house after work.'

'You'd better make sure you get a pretty special husband,' I would snort.

Whenever we had that conversation I could envision Jay, flushed and beautiful, surrounded by kids and a loving husband, bringing laughter and service to everyone who met her. My future for Jasmine was almost as concrete as the one I had for myself. I just didn't realise how entwined they were. If I had been the one with the tumour she would still have lived her ideal life, her best life. Instead, she's in hospital and my future has been dashed away with hers.

Not dashed, I correct myself. Simply altered. God still works for good… For the first time it really hits me. My idea of God working for good had been this: Our lives are disrupted for a little while, we all learn some lessons and Grow As People, and then normality returns and we live on.

'That's not going to happen, Lord, is it? Nothing is going to be the same again.' I burst into tears. Another thing showers are brilliant for is crying. If I cry in the shower I'm never left with suspicious red track marks or puffy eyes. 'I just wanted to go rural. That's all I ever, ever wanted! And now – now—'

I know life isn't ideal, Lord. I know that. But aren't I allowed to weep for what will never be? I'm going to have to be Jasmine now, aren't I? I'm going to have to do everything she was going to do – I can't build my future on top of hers anymore. I clench my fists. 'I don't want to!' The words grate against my throat, low and guttural. 'I don't *want* to be Jasmine. I'm no good at it. She's good at being herself, and you've taken that away!'

I double over and the stream of water hits the back of my neck, wetting my hair. Will I ever get used to my new future? It feels like my stomach will seal itself into hot knots before I get the chance. I cry with my mouth open until the tepid water splatters against my tonsils. I don't know if I can leave this shower. A world without my future in it isn't very appealing.

'You're being ridiculous.' To my surprise my voice is raw but calm. 'You're allowed to be sad, but it's not the end of everything.'

The jury people mutter and nudge each other. Finally, one steam-cloaked figure stands up. *You've made the right decision, and you're also right in saying that it's not the end of the world. But it feels like that to you, and that's okay.*

'But I don't *want* crying to be okay! I don't *want* ruined futures to be okay! I don't *want* sisters facing open brain surgery to be okay!'

At that the jury dissipates. They're great proponents of logic and reason, but in this shower I need more than that.

'Help me Jesus,' I beg. 'Help me to get used to this unideal world. You know what it's like. And please, please work a miracle, because I'm so sad. Even though I have to stay, can I somehow get a job at a rural hospital? Somehow?'

My phone rings and I stare at it. Any of the other students on the uni lawn would assume I'm deciding whether to answer it. In reality, I'm gathering up the courage to do so. *Help me Lord.*

'Hello, this is the Base Hospital Radiology Department for your phone interview. You're speaking to—'

'Hi, it's Emily.' At once any courage I had fades. 'I just wanted to say I won't be doing the interview because my sister has a brain tumour and I want to find a job near her.'

Silence. I don't imagine it's an excuse they hear very often.

'Oh. Sorry to hear that. All the best.' *Click*.

I pocket my phone and stand there for a moment. Time to apply to some of the city hospitals, I guess. The idea of securing a position in one of those places feels equal to that of getting invited to tea with the Prime Minister. *Private practice it is for you, Emily.*

If nothing else, it will be a lesson in perseverance.

Operation Eight

DIARY EXCERPT
November 9, 2015 (56 days in hospital)

Tomorrow Jasmine is having her 8th operation. It's going to be big and they're already planning what to do if it fails. That hurts.

Chapter Nineteen: In the Depths of the Earth

I run up the stairs. It's odd, this hospital thing.

In the past 59 days I've spent more one-to-one time with Jasmine than the last seventeen years. You think I'd be satiated from that much sisterly presence, but instead I miss her. It's been three days since they opened up her skull to fix her leak. Three days since I've laid eyes on her. Three days since she survived for the eighth time...

It's the longest I've spent away from the hospital since she was admitted.

'Hey, Jay!' I'm a bit afraid, although no-one, I hope, would be able to tell from my expression. They said the operation went 'well' — but if I've learned one thing it's this: the meaning of that four-letter word is extremely relative.

Mum smiles from across the room, her skin looking particularly tanned next to the white blob in the bed. 'Heey.' The white blob calls. I dump my bags and hurry to the bed.

Mum and I do a handover. We're very efficient; we have had a lot of practice. Once she leaves I turn to the white blob. 'I've missed you so much.' The bedrail is down so I lean over and give her a gentle hug. She returns it, hands fluttering like butterflies against my spine. 'So much,' I murmur and breathe in the scent of soft skin and bed-sweat and stale antiseptic. I want to stay like this forever.

'I love you,' she says.

I smile into her neck and enjoy the novelty of those words. 'I love you too.' I reply, and hold her tighter.

'Oww.' She moans, wiggling back. 'You're hot.'

I take a seat on the chair beside her. 'How long does your head have to be all wrapped up for?'

Jay shrugs. 'I dunno. It hurts.' She touches her eyebrow. 'Here. Throbs.'

I wince in sympathy. 'Look! I went to that Asian bakery. You know, the yummy one? I got the softest, fluffiest bread I could find, 'cause I figured you'd be in too much pain to chew.'

'Yum.' She does smile, but it's so faint an eraser could wipe it off. The plaits poking out of her bandage look like antennas. Each time the doctors operate they add something. Fat from her stomach or her leg, sterile packaging, gauze, drains, shunts – but they must also scrape something away. It's the only explanation I have for why she seems so wraith-like in this place.

'Mum said you had an interview today,' she says gently. 'How did it go?'

Ah yes. The reason it's 3 pm and I've only just arrived. The reason I've been MIA for the last two days. The reason I woke up ridiculously early today and drove forty minutes and took two buses only to arrive at a hospital which didn't contain Jasmine. I shrug. 'It was okay. The spoken questions were fine. I could tell the interviewers were agreeing-nodding. Then they pulled out x-rays for critique and I gave a stupid wrong answer and it sort of went downhill. They began listening-nodding instead.'

'Ah.' It's Jasmine's turn to wince in sympathy. Or actually, it could have been a real pain-wince. It's hard to tell.

'It's alright.' I shrug again. 'They interview so many people; I don't expect to get a job there anyway. It was good practice.'

It's true. I don't care. Now I've made the decision not to go rural, these interviews are all steps to follow. I can't imagine working at any of these hospitals, just as I can't imagine a life when Jasmine is *not* in a hospital. I'm living in two worlds. The one with the white blob on the bed is the real one, and the other with interview nerves and stressed peers and endless typed applications is only a dream.

Jasmine groans. 'Is it time for more Panadol yet?'

'I dunno. When did they last come around?'

'Ages ago!' She bursts into tears.

'Here,' I say in my low, calm, everything-is-just-fine-and-dandy-really voice. 'Press the buzzer.'

The Nurse Assist light goes on. We wait. And wait. 'Arghhh...' she groans again. 'My head is on fire.' She begins to pant, eyes closed, chest arching. 'Make it stop!'

'I would if I could.'

'Go get the nurse,' she bites her lip. 'It hurts so much!'

'I'm sure she's on her way.' I twist in my seat and peer through the open door. There's no one in the hallway. 'I can see your light blinking at the nurses' station.'

'Ow! Please.'

'What sort of pain is it?' I try to delay. If her pain relief medication isn't due she won't get any, and I'm in no hurry to deal with the fall-out.

'Pain!' she hisses and she's gone. The girl who hugged me is crying and bucking, consumed with the burning, pounding, throbbing, clanging in her skull. *Oh Lord, help.*

A nurse bustles in. She fits the term 'matron' exactly. The stout, busy, I've-been-doing-this-since-before-you-were-born type. If she steps around to my side of the bed I'm sure I'll see varicose veins and black rubber clogs. 'Jasmine, is it? You pressed your buzzer.'

'She's in a lot of pain,' I say. 'Can she have more pain relief?'

The nurse does a sort of squat. It looks painful. Her head comes to rest level with Jasmine's. 'What's wrong?' she asks.

Oh. She's the sort who likes the patient to answer. I'm normally that sort too, but again Jasmine somehow manages to be the exception to all my ideals.

'My head,' Jay whimpers. 'It's stabbing. Above my eyebrow.'

'Hmm.' The nurse straightens. 'You've got yourself all worked up.' She places a large hand on Jasmine's forehead.

'Oww!'

'That's where it hurts!' I'm on my feet. Fists clenched. Just give her some pain relief. Please. I'll get down on my knees if I have to.

'Hmm,' she says again. 'You haven't had pain relief that long ago.' She looks back at Jasmine. 'You really are getting all sweaty.' She moves away and returns with a blood pressure cuff. 'Let me check your blood pressure.'

Jasmine moans. 'So can she have pain relief?' I ask.

'Let me check the blood pressure,' the nurse repeats. If she thinks we've reached a compromise, she's mistaken. I don't take my eyes off Jasmine's sweating, stone-coloured face while the cuff thrums. *Derr. Derr. Derr.* A mechanical sigh. The spell breaks. I release my gaze. The nurse looks up at the reader. Her eyebrows rise. 'See! Look how high it is! You need to take some deep breaths.'

'Is it time yet?' Jasmine begs. 'Can I have more Panadol?'

The nurse frowns. 'I will have a look. We have to be careful you know. If we give you too much we'll have trouble on our hands.' The implication is clear. If they give her too much pain relief, they'll relieve her of more than her pain. Life is fragile, and nowhere is that more understood than a children's hospital ward.

Jay bursts into a terrified wail as the nurse leaves. I struggle not to storm after her and demand she take back her words in a world which is hard enough without black coercion and pointless warnings.

'It's okay, Jay. She's going to get you something.' I say instead, and pray that it's true.

It's like a tomb in here.

'Don't you want *some* light at least?'

Jasmine moans a negative. At least that's my assumption. It's a pretty good one – there haven't been any positive moans for a while. I sit back on the plastic chair by her bed. It's a repeat of yesterday but twelve times worse, as if we've descended down several circles in Dante's hell. It's not an inappropriate picture really. Save for that one horrific night in Recovery, this is the worst I've seen her.

'Do you want me to tell you a story? Or I can read…' I almost insert the title of her English text, but stop myself just in time, '… something?' I'm desperate to help. Desperate to fix this. Somehow. Anyhow.

A negative moan. Her stretched-out body shivers. A tiny sliver of light from the joining of the window and blind picks out the bubbles of sweat on her skin. Her hair looks as dark as mine in this light, soaked through and stuck to her forehead, twirling in lank curls around her ears.

'How about you try and sleep?'

'Noooooo!' She thrashes.

'What is it? What's wrong?'

'Dreams.' She whispers up at me. One eye is wide and staring. The other is red, half shut, the bandages covering her eyebrow.

Dreams? That's new. 'What sort of dreams?' I edge forward in my seat, as close as I can get to the bed without slipping in beside her. 'Last night?'

Her head twitches in affirmation. She can't nod anymore. Pain has stripped her of the ability to do anything but lie on her back and moan. 'What did you dream?' I repeat. 'Nightmares?'

'I know they're not real,' she whispers. Did she catch the softening in my voice, or is she trying to convince herself? 'But they're yucky.'

'Yucky?' Did she dream of vomit and boogers? I wait.

She arches on the bed in un-voiced pain. When the spasm is over, her one good eye searches me out. 'It's like I'm in the air,' she whispers. 'And I look down and I can see *me*. Except I'm all…' she closes her staring eye briefly. '… broken.'

Broken?

'There's blood everywhere. And I can feel it. It's warm and sticky and I'm lying in a big pool of it. I'm dying.'

Woah. And here I thought I was going to have to reassure her that monsters don't hide under hospital beds.

'Sometimes I'm missing legs or arms,' she continues. 'So much blood.'

I swallow.

'There's sharks too.'

Can this get any worse?

'And a waterfall which I keep falling off. From the top of the rocks to the ground. Then there's more blood.'

Yes it can.

'The sharks chase me and eat me. Sometimes it happens before I even close my eyes. I can see them and me and I know it's not real but I keep forgetting. It's so easy to forget.' Her voice drones on through the shadows, bereft of inflection. Bereft of anything that resembles life. I feel like I'm sitting with her in the bowels of the underworld, waiting. For what? Not death. Not on my watch.

'Jay, that's awful.' My voice cracks. 'That's really awful. I'm going to get a nurse.' I don't even bother with a buzzer. Just stride into the corridor and grab the first one I find. 'Please, Jasmine is having awful dreams. Really awful ones. With blood. And now she doesn't want to sleep. Is it one of her medications?'

She frowns. 'Hallucinations can be a side effect of ketamine,' she puts a hand in the pocket of her navy scrubs. 'One second and I'll be right in.'

As I watch her retreating head I realise there are reindeer antlers perched on top. Is it Christmas? Here I was thinking it was Halloween. *Hallucinations*. I prefer Jasmine's term: 'bad dreams'. Hallucinations happen to crazy people. Or really, really sick, dying people like my Opa who saw giant spiders before he died. Jasmine's not that sick. *Is she?* I re-enter the room.

'Hello!' It's Aunty Berna and my uncle too. That's right, I remember. Uncle Jerry has a job nearby. They were going to visit and bring a Boost Juice to tempt Jay into eating something. Sure enough, Jasmine's clutching the icy-cold beverage in both hands like Ophelia holding her funeral flowers. Her eyes are closed, but whether in ecstasy or sleep I can't tell.

'Hello.' I want to cry. *Adults*. I forgot how calming they are. They don't even have to *do* anything, and they still manage to exude a reassuring presence. Just to see Aunty Berna sitting here, real, warm, solid, is a reminder of the existence of another world. One where the sun is shining, where some people are healthy and well. As Jay said, 'it's so easy to forget'. Is this how Lazarus felt when Jesus broke his tomb open? Did that first mouthful of sweet air make him dizzy with nostalgia and hope? 'She's in a lot of pain. I just got the nurse.'

Aunty Berna pushes her chair back so I can get through. Jay moans at the noise and the juice straw slips from her mouth and spills a yellow trail down her chin. Aunty Berna rescues it. 'Do you want me to hold it while you suck? No. Okay, I'll put it here for now.'

'Sick.' The bed shakes. 'No more.'

Aunty Berna holds it out to me. 'Do you want some?'

I pull at the straw. Sweet icy slush storms into my mouth. It tastes better than anything I've ever had. It reminds me of summer and warmth and painless people.

'… do you think?'

'Sorry?' I meet Aunty Berna's concerned eyes. Here I am mooning over mango juice, while she's speaking to me adult-to-adult. Deferring to my opinion, as if I specialised in Jasmine Studies, not Applied Science. I need to concentrate.

'Her eye. Do you think it's swollen? Could the pain be due to an infection?'

That's a good theory. Why wasn't it mine? 'Maybe...' I put the drink down and tiptoe to the other side of the bed. Jasmine's eyes remain closed. 'I sort of just thought it was normal, the result of the operation... but you're right. This whole side of her face looks swollen.' Deformed and red. *Broken.* I thrust Jay's description away. I need to get a grip. However absolutely, horrendously, unimaginably *awful* this is, I need to—

'Jasmine?'

It's the nurse. 'She's asleep,' I say, in case it's not obvious. It's so dark in here, we may as well be swapping eulogies around an empty casket for all anyone can see.

'Does she look swollen to you?' Aunty Berna asks, in a wonderfully adult voice. Where can I buy one like that?

'On the left side?' The nurse considers, fiddling with her stethoscope. Her green felt antlers cast weird horn-like silhouettes across Jasmine's slack skin. She places a gentle hand on Jay's head. 'She feels a bit hot. Could be a bone infection. I think I'll ring the team.'

'And pain relief? She's in so much pain.' I promise. Even if at the moment she looks blissfully angelic (well, if you pretend the bandages are a halo and the swelling and stitches are beauty spots). Please believe me. If I have to listen to another hour of moaning I think I'll have a breakdown.

'Hmm,' the nurse considers. 'Jasmine. Jasmine, are you awake?'

Don't! Too late. Jay stirs and moans. She begins to cry. I glare at the nurse. See what you've done?

'Hey sweetie. How are you feeling?'

Clearly ten out of ten. That's why there are tears running down her stitches and collecting in the bruises beneath her eyes.

'Hurts. Sharp. Throbbing.' She bucks against the bed sheets.

'Where? Where does it hurt?'

'Eye. Forehead. Head.' She groans.

'And you're having nightmares.'

'Yes.' It's a whispered sigh. 'Of blood.'

'Must be the ketamine.' The nurse trundles an obs machine out of the corner. 'I'll check her temperature. Perhaps she's allergic. The redness looks a bit hive-like to me. Hmm. I'm going to make a call.' She stops at the foot of the bed, blonde ponytail swinging beneath green antlers. 'Just try and rest sweetie.' There's a shuddering sigh from the bed and a low moan.

Ten minutes goes by. The nurse re-appears. 'The team want Jasmine to have a CT scan in case there are complications causing her pain, a wardsman will come in the next half hour.' She smiles. *Complications.* How I hate that word.

Uncle Jerry leaves for his job. Moan. Aunty Berna eats her lunch. Moan. Aunty Berna tries to get me to eat the lunch she brought me. Moan. Jasmine drifts off to sleep. No moans. 'Aghh!'

I jump to my feet. Aunty Berna's warm body is beside me. 'What is it? What's wrong?'

'A shark. There! Ooohh..'

I moan.

'We're going to take her for a CT.'

What? You mean that's actually happening? I'd given up hope. It's been two hours. 'Okay.' I stagger to my feet.

Aunty Berna manages to find me in the shadows. 'Do you want me to come?'

'It's okay. It shouldn't be too long.' I smile. I'm a radiographer after all. I've done CTs myself. The wardsman has trouble manoeuvring Jasmine's bed out of the ward and it bumps against the wall.

'Ooohh!' Jasmine screams.

'It's okay – it's okay.' We leave the ward. Bump goes the bed. Moan goes Jasmine. Throb goes my heart. 'It's okay.' Bump goes the bed. Moan goes Jasmine. Throb goes my heart. 'It's okay.'

It's a very long way to Radiology.

'Nooo!! I'm falling!' She sits up as they transfer her onto the CT table. 'The shark's got me!'

I stare at the computer screens from behind the safety barrier. They won't stop swimming around. If I straighten my chin the radiographers can't see my face, but then gravity is against me and it's harder to keep my tears from collecting on my jaw. I straighten my shoulders instead. Just keep staring. No one will want to chat if you look like a human icicle. Only one tear leaks out the entire length of the scan. Crisis averted.

Bump. Moan. 'It's okay.' The corridor stretches out relentlessly. I hate blue carpet with all of my heart.

'Hello, I'm from the Pain Team.' Unfamiliar staff flood into the room and congregate around Jay's bed. The speaker is tall and clean shaven and looks like Sherlock Holmes from the ink sketches circa 1895. He could have been bald with pimples the size of satellite dishes and I wouldn't have cared.

'Thank you.' No really, *thank you*. At last, someone to help us! Someone to—

'She's on a lot of drugs at the moment.' He looms over Jasmine from the foot of the bed. His people shuffle papers and look curious. One types on a portable computer. Where did *that* come from?

'I know, but they're not working.' Look at her! Is it normal to have a face that grey? Do you normally see someone sleeping with a grimace on their lips? 'They think the ketamine is giving her hallucinations.'

He doesn't look up. 'I'm guessing you're not her mother.'

'I'm her older sister.'

'...So where is she?'

I swallow. 'She's not well. She's at home.'

He spins. *'You're* not her mother?'

'Her mother's sister,' Aunty Berna replies and leans forward in her chair by the bedhead. 'I know Jasmine very well.'

He looks back at me. 'Are you here often?'

'Every second day. Sometimes more.' I'm desperate to convince him I can be trusted. 'I'm twenty-one. I signed the consent for her surgery—'

'She's on too much pain medication.'

My jaw drops.

'You need to open the curtain,' he stalks to the side of the bed. 'It's too dark.'

'The light was causing her too much pain. It was hurting her eyes.'

'Jasmine? Jasmine?' She wakes with a jerk. For a second her good eye is clear and then it clouds with pain. She begins to cry. 'See?' he turns to me. 'It's too dark.'

What?

'Jasmine, where does it hurt?'

'My head...' she moans. 'Here.'

He bends over her. Why did I ever think he looked like Sherlock Holmes? He's definitely Dracula. 'Let's forget the pain for a moment,' he says, voice softening from granite to sandstone. 'What do you like doing, Jasmine?'

I thought you were a Pain Doctor, not a Recreational Therapist. She groans. 'Nothing.'

'And how is your appetite?'

'Not hungry.'

'She's been drinking Boost Juice,' Aunty Berna says. 'She's in too much pain for anything else.'

Dracula ignores her. 'Are you looking forward to going home, Jasmine?' She doesn't answer. 'Hmmm.' He straightens. 'Right. We need the curtains up to let in some light. Then we need distraction...'

No. I can see what you're doing. Don't you dare try to slide your way into an easy diagnosis. You're a pain doctor, not a psych. I push my nails into the palms of my hands. I know why you're asking those questions. Don't think I don't.

Once I cried for three days. I felt like I was wrapped in cling wrap and the only way I dragged myself out of the house was by singing hymns loud enough to drown out a voice that may as well have belonged to the third rider of the apocalypse, the way it tried to convince me that everything was pointless and nothing mattered. I know exactly what you're asking, *doctor*.

Stop. Breathe. I can't let him dismiss me. It's just me standing between him and Jasmine. If I use the wrong words, if I can't convince him to listen... wait a second. I'm not alone. Aunty Berna's in the corner. But she's not saying anything? Why? Could it be – could it be that she trusts me?

'She's not depressed.' I give the doctor a moment for that to sink in. 'She's crying because she's in pain. She can't think of anything in the future because she's in too much pain. It's dark in here because otherwise she's in *more* pain.' So fix the *pain* and I promise you *doctor*, her mood will improve. I know exactly how pain affects people. I've watched Mum for two decades. It's miraculous how chipper one feels when there's no rogue hammer trying to smash one's cerebrum to smithereens.

'What about her – *your* – mum?'

Not this again. She's at home, I told you. She's not well. I swallow the bubble threatening to burst in my throat. 'What do you mean?'

'You said she was unwell. Is this a regular event? Are these just physical illnesses? Is she generally a happy person?'

Has she got depression? Is that what you mean? 'She, she has a lot of chronic illnesses,' I straighten my shoulders. 'Anyone like that is not going to be happy all the time, but she's not...' That's it. That's done it. It's all your fault *Pain-in-my-neck Doctor*. I can talk about Jasmine or I can talk about Mum – but I *can't* talk about them both. I gag deep in my oesophagus and my eyes overflow.

'Their mother's very resilient,' Aunty Berna says.

'Hmm...' The doctor looks at Jasmine. 'I don't really want to put her on drugs to improve her mood. She's a bit young.'

'She doesn't need—' I'm blinded by hot, furious tears. Which is better? To speak and cry harder, or to stay silent and hope they'll stop? I turn my face away, pretending I'm checking on Jasmine. He'll never listen to me now! Crying like a child. I've ruined everything—

'Are you okay?' Aunty Berna moves close. Her voice is maternal. There's no other word for it. But she can't be maternal, because I *can't* be a child—

'Right. Well, I'll chart her a different medication in place of the ketamine and I'll make her team aware.' Dracula nods at me.

Go on. Comment on my tears. I dare you!

'Try and keep the curtains open as much as possible.' Just like that he's gone, his entourage wrestling their computer-on-wheels into the corridor. Good riddance. Oh, *good riddance.* I fall into my chair. One sob escapes before I can catch it.

'Are you okay?' Jasmine whispers.

Aunty Berna is still on her feet. She crosses her arms firmly, staring at the departing team. 'Some people just *don't* listen.'

A slightly hysterical giggle escapes through my tears.

I collapse against the car seat. Rain crawls across my windscreen. The puddles on the pavement dance with five o'clock shadows and the remnants of other people's energy. Red, yellow and green sluices from the traffic lights and collects in concentric circles on the bitumen. Why is the rain so beautiful? My sister's whimpering in a dark room and the water droplets look like precious stones.

I can't do this. I can't watch her in pain anymore.

You have given me strength so far Lord, it's true — but now I want out. I don't care if you've got a plan for all of this. No 'good' can possibly make it all worth it. I just want it to stop.

I don't even care if every person in the hospital comes to understand who you truly are because of this. I don't care. Stop this. End it all. You can flatten the roof of the hospital and squash us all like empty tin cans. You have my permission, Lord.

I've had enough.

All the bad things

DIARY EXCERPT
November 20, 2015 (67 days in hospital)

My interview was... okay...I'm so tired now. The adrenaline's petering out and leaving me with a sister whose nose began dripping again today, and more long and weary days ahead and no hope of relief on the horizon. When will it end?...I question and cry and beg... Oh Lord, glorify your name.

'Don't call me Naomi,' she told them. 'Call me Mara, because the Almighty has made my life very bitter.'
Ruth 1:10 (NIV)

Untitled

DIARY EXCERPT
November 21, 2015 (68 days in hospital)

Oh Lord. When will it end?
More drains.
More surgery.
More pain.
More sadness.
'Suffocating night,' Victor Hugo calls it.
… I don't know what to say… I don't understand.

REFLECTION
Our goal is not peace

What's your goal in troubled times? We're often told that it's okay to simply *survive*, yet most of us, if we're completely honest, want more than that.

We want to turn something bad into something good. Something worthwhile. Maybe even something precious. There's a reason so many cancer tragedies end in the formation of an organisation or charity. There's a reason we prefer tales of people who have overcome illness, rather than the much more common stories of *being* overcome.

Christians talk a lot about peace. So much so that it's easy to feel like you're doing something wrong if you're not an unflappable yogi during trials. Yet the reality is, our goal in tragedy is not to 'keep calm and carry on'. Why? Firstly, because unless you're a natural Pollyanna, that's going to be impossible. Second, because being stoic does not change something bad into something good. It might make it easier to *survive* for a short while, but we want more than that. We want to look back at the dark days and say *they were done well.*

So how do we live through disaster *well?* We take our terrifying anxieties and our aching sadnesses in both hands and we look heavenward. We choose to let despair draw us to Jesus, rather than away. We decide to live rightly during periods of sleeplessness and chaos. We recite our worldview over and over to our numb hearts until we find meaning in what is meaningful.

Jesus is king over this darkness.

Jesus is choosing to let me go through this for a reason and a purpose.

Jesus has my best interests at heart.

One day I will look back on my life, and I will see all my shadowy valleys gilded with the gold of a new Day dawning. I will behold a glorious picture which would have been impossible if my journey had taken place on a smooth, flat plain. On that last evening I will realise that I have been made beautiful *because* Jesus led me over perilous mountain passes and through suffocating gorges, not in spite of them.

Our goal is not physical peace during agony and illness. Despair and fear does not mean you've failed in this walk called life. Rather, every emotion can be redeemed if we let it pull us towards Jesus.

It's not sinful to struggle in the face of affliction. Jesus was troubled before his death – did that mean he did not trust God enough? So many Christians have lived through immense hardship, and they have not come out unmarked – but they *have* come out more like Jesus.

I think of William Wilberforce, who suffered from nervous breakdowns each time his bill to end slavery was defeated. I think of Martin Luther who often felt driven to distraction by worry over his salvation, his teachings and his congregation. I think of Charles Spurgeon who struggled to find joy in the midst of ongoing depression.

I use these big names because they are well known, but there are so, so many more in the annals of history, many of which have left no mark at all in this world, save this: they were faithful with what they had been given. They struggled, they failed, they reached out to Jesus, and they tried to love their neighbour.

What more can we ask, than to be able to look back on dark days and hear Jesus say, *you lived them well, good and faithful friend?* This, not physical feelings of peace or joy, will be what redeems our tragedy. This, not simply *surviving,* will be what forms our crown. **And 'this' is within everyone's reach: all he asks is that we seek him one dark day at a time.**

PART FOUR

Chapter Twenty-one: To Hope Again

'Jay?'

'Mmm?' She watches me from under half-closed eyelids. Her hair is frazzled from the braids she's worn since her last surgery.

'If you wake up and I'm not here, just text.' I hold my phone up. 'I'll have it with me.'

'Where are you going?' Her eyes close further. She has been dozing off all day. Probably a side effect of the strong antibiotics pumping through her thin wrist. Still, there are worse side effects.

Shark hallucinations, for instance.

'Do you hear that?' I gesture at the plaster behind her head. The noise is muffled but unmistakable. Whatever else hospital walls are, they are *not* soundproof. Someone – or rather some *people*, by the sounds of it – are singing. And not just any songs, but tunes I recognise.

Hymns. It's Sunday afternoon and someone's holding a church service. 'I might join.' Depending on how you react to this announcement.

'Cool.' She's wonderfully, remarkably, unconcerned. Her pain is dropping; her face isn't as swollen. It's incredible what receiving the correct diagnosis (meningitis) and the correct treatment (something more potent than simply opening windows) can do. The Pain Doctor hasn't made a reappearance, but there are times I wish he would, just so I can tell him how wrong he was. Even the drips from Jay's nose have settled now they've put another lumbar drain in. Most excitingly, the light isn't hurting her eyes and sometimes she giggles.

She is asleep a second later. Perhaps I should do the same. A quick nap... No. I can't settle. There's something about that music. When was the last time I was in church? It's grabbing at me, pulling me, drawing me in... I'm so hungry. Not for food, but for... what? *Jesus*. I check my phone is on loud and step out into the corridor. Just follow the music, how difficult can it be?

The notes lead me to the doors of the common room. I remember Jasmine's surprise party and wonder what awaits me on the other side. Her birthday feels like eons ago. Today the double doors are closed, but luckily they're the sort with windows. I lift myself onto my toes, rest my hand on the wood and pull myself to the height of the glass.

Only to discover that someone inside has drawn the curtains. I suppose I'll just have to barge right in. Sorry folks, heard your singing. Can't carry a tune to save my life, but thought it'd be a brilliant idea if I joined. Hope you don't mind! Is that polite? I realise it doesn't matter. This is Hospital, not the real world. Here social norms have a habit of getting left by the wayside. Besides, if nothing else, these people are my kin. Their songs sing of the realities which flow through my blood. No forget that. These realities are my life blood: Everything else has been ripped away.

I push open the door.

Fifteen people and one guitar. They're quite young. My age, give or take five years. Except for those two. They look older. Parent-age. I've seen them somewhere before... Oh. They're Oscar's parents. Oscar shared a room with Jasmine for a while. He's... well, he's worse. I don't think he'll ever walk again. Or talk, or... anything much.

They're sitting in a circle on the floor. I guess they're a youth group of some kind. I step forward and squat down. 'Hey.' I try my best not to disrupt the song. 'I thought I'd join.' The girl besides me smiles and shuffles over. I lower myself down and the cement is hard and cold. I place my phone where I can see it. *'...through many dangers, toils and snares, we have already come.'* I sing. Across from me a boy nudges his neighbour who relinquishes a battered hymnal.

The book makes its way around the circle until it reaches the girl on my left. 'Here,' she says. 'Do you know the words?'

I smile. 'Yeah, but thanks.'

'...*Grace has brought us safe thus far, and grace will lead us home.*'

A brief silence. The guitarist strums, lengthening some old notes and adding new ones. The circle swells and breaks into song.

'*Oh the deep, deep love of Jesus, vast, unmeasured, boundless, free!*' The words fall off my tongue. How many times have I sung this song? Ten? Twenty times? Fifty? One hundred? Yet how often have I sung it on the floor of a hospital with fifteen scruffy youth and a collection of green-covered hymn-books?

Not often enough. '*...underneath me, all around me, is the current of Thy love...*' Love, even here. Sixty-eight days later. '*How He loveth, ever loveth, changeth never, nevermore! How He watches o'er His loved ones—*'

Watch over her, Lord. Bring Jay home.

'*... Jesus, love of every love the best. 'Tis an ocean full of blessing, 'tis a haven giving rest!*'

This is better than a nap. This is soul nourishing, hope restoring. I've never met these people, we've exchanged about seven words in total, but I've never felt more comfortable.

'... And it lifts me up to glory, for it lifts me up to Thee!'

The song peters out, but the thickness in the air remains. I'm really not one for 'spiritual experiences', but this? This is special. Brief interludes like these, glimpses of heaven, they take my breath away. They give me hope again. Not in healing. Not even in discharge. But in you, my God.

'Quick, it's melting!' I thrust the thick-shake at the bed and drop my bags to the floor. 'I was so scared it would be a puddle before I got here. It's good, isn't it?'

Jay takes a sip and smiles. 'Mmm... so good.'

I pull on my own straw, fingers soaking up the moisture on the outside of the plastic cup. 'It's so hot out there. I reckon it's going to reach forty-five degrees again this afternoon.'

Jay gives a sudden shiver. 'Brr... ow!'

'What is it?'

A crooked grin. 'Brain freeze.'

I smirk. 'Well, it doesn't help that you're still not allowed to sit up. The cold has nowhere to go.'

Her right eyebrow does a flutter. 'Yeah, 'cause that sounds scientific.'

I snigger. 'I can't take you seriously with that eyebrow.'

She wrinkles her nose. 'I think I need eyebrow strengthening exercises. Y'know, to help the numbness wear off.'

'Yeah, 'cause that's scientific.' We laugh. 'Guess what?' I continue. 'I used my phone to find a Hungry Jacks and it was connected to a petrol station!'

'So?'

'So? Have you ever seen that before? It's amazing. There was this big building and half was a petrol station and half was Hungry Jacks.'

'Wow, amazing.' She deadpans.

I roll my eyes. 'It is! When you're better we're going to go there.'

Her eyebrow flutters. 'And what, get petrol?'

'No! Hungry Jacks! Although actually, we could get both, since this place is so amazing—'

'I'm cold.' Jay holds out her plastic cup.

I take it before I can process what I'm doing, and then I stop. The world tilts. Somehow I've just reacted unconsciously to Jay's unspoken need, my body moving in sync with hers. She held out her hand, supremely confident in my ability to fix the situation, and I did, naturally, almost absently. As if it was normal, as if it was *right*.

Is this how parents feel? Equal parts responsible, determined, and inadequate? It's a warm but heady mixture. The thick-shake sweats against my palm. I push it onto the rolling table, and try and straighten the world. 'What have you done to this straw – mutilated it?'

She pokes her tongue out, eyes closed. I swallow another beautifully cool mouthful and feel the moisture sticking my singlet top to my back begin to dry.

'Blanket.'

I pull it up to her shoulders, making sure it doesn't snag on either her drains or her cannula. 'Happy?'

She smiles.

'Obs time!' A round shouldered nurse sweeps into the room, dragging the portable blood pressure cuff behind her. 'You look sleepy, lovey.'

Jay pries open her eyes. I look up from my interview notes.

'Sorry, it's going to be a bit cold. There.' The nurse slips the blue cuff up Jay's arm. 'Did you tell your sister about your exciting morning?'

'No?' I put down my papers. 'What happened?'

'Ooh, that's right! I forgot.' Jasmine's wide awake now, face flushed. 'These people came and they had photos with us and they were from Sydney CSF.'

'*CSF?*' Cerebral Spinal Fluid and I are well acquainted. It's the bane of my existence, the thing leaking out of Jasmine's nose and the reason she's still in hospital.

'Oooh!' Jasmine bursts into laughter. The blood pressure machine squeals. 'I meant *SFC*. Sydney Football Club! I think I have CSF on the brain.'

The nurse meets my eyes. 'Literally!' we exclaim together, and collapse in laughter. It's a long time before anyone goes back to sleep, work or study. As I pick up my notes I realise our laughter is more than a reaction to a word mix-up. It's a testament to how long it's been since Jasmine has leaked.

It's a sign we're beginning to hope again.

Chapter Twenty-two: A Last Ditch Attempt

'Didn't feel like raisin toast this morning?' The breakfast tray with its plastic plate and paper packaged cutlery lays untouched on her rolling table.

'Bread.' Jay says in a dull voice. She pulls her smiling, blue, plush toy brain, a gift from her school friends, to her chest. 'Raisin *bread*. No toasters in hospital.'

I shove my bags into the corner. 'What's wrong?'

'I'm fasting.'

'Oh no.' I launch towards the bed. A hug. I can do a hug.

'Go away!' She flails.

I slump back into the plastic chair. 'I thought...' Calm, stay calm. 'I thought the drain was working?'

'Well it's not! Nothing ever works.' Jay stares up at the ceiling. 'I had to collect a sample from my nose last night... and it tested positive. It's CSF.'

I push my thumbnails into the softest part of my fingers. Pain, that's what I need. Then I won't wail. Then I won't throw a temper tantrum. *Ouch*. There we go. Oh dear, this isn't going to work. I can feel despair bubbling in my chest, my oesophagus, my throat... The moment passes.

'When's the op?' I speak with less inflection than a self-serve checkout machine at the supermarket. How can I raise Jay's morale when mine is barely floating?

'My team's in surgery so I'm fasting in case they want to operate when they come out.'

If I thought my voice was listless, well, Jay's takes the word to a whole new level. 'I'm sorry, Jay. I... I really am.'

Silence.

'Ask them when the surgery is.'

I sigh. 'I've asked them. Multiple times. No one knows. They can't contact your team.'

'I'm so thirsty.'

'I know.' I try and dredge up sympathy. If I were her, I'd... no. Don't go there. 'How about we play a game?'

'I don't want to play a game.'

'Not even I Spy?'

She rolls her eyes. 'I'm hungry.'

'We can collect themes for your English module?'

'Can't concentrate. Too thirsty.'

'Or make a study timetable for Community and Family Studies?'

'What's the point? My operation's this afternoon. By the time I've recovered, I'll have forgotten everything.'

An annoyingly good point. How is she ever going to complete her HSC? The first term is almost over and we've read two English texts and glanced at her Community Studies textbook. That's it. 'Listen to your audiobook.'

'It makes me feel sick.'

'How can an audiobook make you feel sick?' This is getting ridiculous.

'I was listening to it when I had a temperature and now I feel yucky when I turn it on.'

'Okay, fine.' I close my own book. 'I'll read to you then. How about—'

'I'm too tired to listen.'

'For goodness sake! Then lie there and stare at the ceiling.'

Silence. 'I'm bored.'

'Then behave like a seventeen-year-old and do something about it.'

'Stop being so patronising! You don't know what it's like! Go away!' I wish I could. I re-open my book on ethics... Who knew the ceiling had so many stains? That one looks like a sheep. Well, sort of. More like a dinosaur.

I'm so bored. 'When did you start fasting?'

'Eight.'

That means she has exactly—

'Five hours to go.' Jay says. Not that either of us is counting.

I open my eyes. It's morning. My room is pale orange. If it's this hot inside it must be at least thirty degrees outside already. I don't want to get up. There's no point anyway, I remember. Not with my brain tumour.

The sheets are stretched tight across my chest. I shuffle. What was I going to do today? Not that it matters. I have a tumour. I'm bound to medications and strapped to specialists. They've forbidden me from living more than thirty minutes from a major hospital, and told me I need to carry replacement hormones everywhere in case of emergency. I close my eyes.

Something's not right. It's like the sudden sizzle of a seat-belt buckle in January. *Oh!* It comes to me in a flash. *I* don't have a brain tumour. But... It must have been a *dream*. I sit up and throw off the sheets. Relief cascades into every part of my body from my neck down to my big toes. Freedom. Independence. Spontaneity...

Guilt. Nausea rolls up my chest. *Jasmine* has the tumour. And the noble thing would be to wish I had it instead. To wish my dream was reality. To beg God for a miraculous transference. I think I'd rather die.

I did it once. Pleaded to God for my Mum's illness. Over and over again, week after week. Let *me* have it, Lord. Save her. Give it to *me*.

One day I stopped. Not because the prayer had been answered, but because I finally understood what I was asking.

It took me years of watching Mum to reach that point, but I was young then. Now I'm old, and far more selfish, and it's only taken me seventy days. Seventy days to build up such a fear of someone else's tragedy that I will not offer my life in exchange, even in the hypothetical.

When I was young I truly believed God might do it, and still I prayed. I would check sometimes, in the early morning, only to find Mum's illnesses in her body and my health in mine, just as it had been when I went to bed.

Now I'm old, and I don't believe God acts in this way, and I'm grateful. This morning relief and guilt tumble through my chest, because Jasmine's sickness is in her body, and my health's in mine, just as it had been when I went to bed. Yet still, I don't pray.

Not for that.

'Right, now obviously we hoped we wouldn't be having this conversation.'

We all nod: Mum, Dad, Jay and I. Three of us in a row, one on a bed.

The neurosurgeon clears his throat. 'As you know, Jasmine's leaking again.' More nods. We're very well trained.

'The previous...' he consults his paperwork, '... eight brain operations and two separate lumbar drain insertion operations have failed to fix her CSF leak.' Nod. Nod. We're a line of wooden marionettes.

'Unfortunately we're running out of options.' How can he say that in front of Jay? 'However, we have spoken to the entire team involved with Jasmine's case, including some international doctors.'

Why is he speaking so slowly? Is he trying to hide the fact that he's telling us nothing new?

'... and we have a new plan.' *Finally.* 'We'll operate on Monday. It will be a joint case between Neurosurgery and Ear, Nose and Throat. The plan is to use fluorescein, a type of dye, and insert it trans-nasally to try and determine the exact location of the leak. We will then mend the leak once more and insert a fourth drain which will remain in place for ten to fourteen days. Then...' He pauses.

Yes? A swallow. Diverted gaze. The surgeon sighs. '...if that doesn't work we will have to try something else.' He doesn't have anything else. That tone of voice... this is a last ditch attempt, isn't it?

'We've never had a case like this before.' He spreads his hands on his knees. They look very tanned against his threadbare scrubs. 'No one's ever had this many failed operations to fix a CSF leak.'

He looks up. I wonder what he thinks of us, sitting in a row. Does he want us to react? Cry? Throw something? We're beyond all that. Nothing can shock us today.

'This procedure on Monday, however... it carries some new risks.'

Again he waits. So do we. Should I say something? Break the silence? When it's just Jay and me I know exactly who I am. Her Adult, her Guardian, her Intercessor. When my parents are present these positions are rightfully theirs, so where does that leave me? Am I adult or child? Essential or superfluous? If I knew my role and had a script I'd play it convincingly.

At last the doctor finds whatever script *he's* been looking for, and speaks. 'This dye... well. If it goes in the wrong place... *well,* it's not the safest procedure. But at the moment it's the best one. It's our only chance of finding this leak. We can go in like all the other times of course and just patch up her nose or insert a drain but so far that hasn't been successful.'

'Will it hurt?' Jasmine's voice is tiny.

'You will be under anaesthetic like all the other times.' It's not a proper answer. Jay's face demonstrates she's well aware of that.

'There's no other way?' Dad asks.

'I'm afraid not. If this doesn't work—'

'Our whole church is praying,' Mum says firmly. 'We are praying for healing.' I wish I had the same confidence.

'Excuse me?'

We jump. The centre of our little tete-a-tete pulls her knees up on the bed.

'Yes, Jasmine?' The surgeon's smile is as cautious as a cat creeping into a new neighbourhood.

'If you're not going to operate today, can I *eat* now? *Please?*'

And with that we're torn from tomorrow's story back into the chapters of today. The surgeon looks confused, and in the background I can almost hear the 'chink' of tracks changing direction. Together we turn away from the monstrosity of an unknown ending and towards Now. And because Now still lives and breathes and is not yet finished, all its unglamorous, inconvenient details are rightly important.

'Er yes, yes of course.' The surgeon blinks. 'No more fasting is, er, necessary, until Monday.'

Jasmine beams.

Chapter Twenty-three: The Surgery That Never Was

Thud, thud, thud. Why is running outside so much more difficult than on a treadmill?

Thud, thud, thud. It's barely eight o'clock and the air is already thicker than a swarm of mosquitoes.

Thud, thud, thud. A yawn jerks me to a stop. I splutter, hands on my hips, looking down into the tree-carpeted valley. Today is Jasmine's ninth brain operation, and eleventh operation in total. Please Lord, heal—

I can't do it. I *can't* pray for healing. I simply don't have the faith. Or the words. Or the energy. Not today. Yet today is the day I need it most! Oh Lord. *Please.* I trust you, Lord. Just... just be with her. Watch over her.

I suck in a breath and launch myself down the hill. *Thud-thud. Thud-thud.*

'What do you *mean* they didn't operate?'

'Shush.' Mum braces her hand against her temple. 'I still have a migraine.'

'*What*,' I hiss, 'do you *mean*, they didn't operate?'

Mum closes her eyes, as if replaying the phone conversation in her head. The phone conversation between Mum and the surgeon. The phone conversation which took place just forty-five minutes after Dad said goodbye to Jasmine in the operating theatre. 'He said they injected the dye and followed the pathway – and there was no leak.'

'What?' No. He's wrong. Doctors get things wrong. I push myself from the dining table. 'Of course there's a leak!'

Mum winces. 'He said there couldn't have been. He said that a leak creates a pathway, and it can't just disappear.'

'She has a leak! She's been leaking for ten weeks!' I splay my hands flat on the plastic tablecloth. 'It tested positive for CSF!'

'I know!' Mum flaps her hands. I can't tell if she's telling me to lower my voice, or joining in my indignation. 'I told him that. I also told him that everyone in our church has been praying for healing.'

Wait, what? 'You said that?' Mum nods with such nonchalance I almost forget we're discussing divine healing and not agreeing that water is wet or the earth is round. I feel like Scrooge. Healing? Bah! Humbug!

Mum's past is pockmarked with the punctures of unanswered prayers and decayed dreams. How can she hope? 'What did the surgeon say?' I demand. What would *I* say, in his place?

Mum flinches and holds her head. 'He said sometimes you come across things that are inexplicable and we just never understand how they happen.'

'And what did you say?'

'*We* know how it happened: God did it.'

'Goodness. Have you ever considered a career as a Christmas tree?'

'Ha ha.' Jay smirks. 'The nurses think it makes me look like an alien.' She sags back against the raised bedhead.

'I can see why.' A tube protrudes from her scalp and hangs for a foot before ending in a collection pouch. Neon yellow fluid runs through the see-through conduit and pools into the bag. It looks like the surgeons have replaced Jasmine's blood with molten highlighter.

'How long will it drain for?'

Jay shrugs. It's amazing how well she looks considering yesterday was operation day. It just goes to show what a difference it makes if your head *hasn't* been cut open recently. 'Till it stops I guess.'

I sit on the edge of the bed. 'How do you feel?'

'Alright. It doesn't hurt much.'

'About them not finding the leak.'

'Oh.' She picks at the tape securing the cannula in her hand. 'Annoyed. I just wanted them to find it and fix it! Now I'm going to leak in a week and I'll have to go through it all over again.'

'Mum says it's a miracle.'

'I know.'

'She thinks you're healed for good.'

'She told me.'

I turn my head. 'You don't think so?'

She sighs. I wonder if my eyes look like that. Ninety-year-old corneas set in a teenager's face. 'No.'

I move over to sit in a chair and give the bed a pat. 'Me neither.'

'I'm turning into you.'

'Huh?' Dad peers up from the lounge room floor. He's lying on his back, arms behind his head. His shaggy eyebrows are sliding off his face.

'Did you sleep here?' I check.

'Not all night. Woke early and couldn't sleep again.' He really does look odd, like something from Picasso, all misshapen features and jagged lines. It must be the result of this particular tincture of grey morning light, offset by the shadow of the green curtains. Fascinating.

I think I'm still half asleep. 'I woke early too.' I tuck my hands under my arms, already too hot in my fluffy dressing gown. It's going to be another scorcher. 'It hits 5 am and bam! I'm awake and then my mind ticks over to Jasmine and I don't sleep again.'

Dad grunts.

'Goodness knows I need the sleep.' I yawn. I need a coffee too. 'Dad?'

'Hmm?'

'Do you think Jay's healed for good?'

He shrugs without removing his hands from behind his head. It brings his Piscasso-ness to a new level. 'Mum thinks so.'

That's not what I asked. 'But what do you think?'

'The doctors said they couldn't find anything.'

That's also not what I asked. I sigh and move towards the kitchen. I'm too tired to rephrase the question. In a way it's sort of nice to think that perhaps I can blame my pessimism on genetics.

Chapter Twenty-Four: Let the Road be Rough and Dreary

I feel like a portable farmers' market. I suspect it's something to do with the boxes of vegetables and bags of fruit cluttering my car. They are all Jasmine's craving at the moment. At least they're not likely to leak across my upholstery and down my leg.

That butter chicken was *not* worth it.

I flip the indicator and sit at the roundabout waiting for an opening. C'mon. There's nothing worse than lukewarm grapes. Here we go! I twist the steering wheel and negotiate the traffic, turning into a narrow road. I ease down on the brakes.

A traffic jam. I stare at the stationary grey car in front of me. I'm so close to the hospital. It would be quicker to walk. The heat belting through the windows intensifies as I idle. Someone really ought to plant some trees along here for shade—

Smash. I plunge my foot on the brake, only to find it's already down as far as it will go. Why am I moving? Something's wrong – *something's wrong*. I've stopped now. What happened? Breathe, don't cry. Why is the car in front of me so close? What was that crunching sound? *What WAS that crunching sound?*

Breathe.

Someone's hit me… I sag against the car seat. And I've hit someone else. *Breathe*. Handbrake. Park. Engine off. Silence. The grapes are definitely going to pickle. They'll taste heavy and sour and *off*. I'll have to—

How bad was the crash? It feels bad. It feels really bad. My stomach returns with a lurch. No! No time to be sick. I turn my neck. One way, then the other. No pain. Good. This is good. I'm not hurt. That's the main thing, right?

What are all those cars doing? Why all the flashing headlights? Oh, lights! I slam my hand down on the dash. My hazard lights blink on. I'm in the middle of the road. I test the ignition. It grumbles with promise, so I hit the indicator. Creep, creep. If I pull over here, can cars get past? Just.

Done. Where's my phone? Keys? I push the door and stagger out. I can walk! Of course you can walk, Emily. It wasn't a head-on crash. Probably felt worse than it actually is. These things always do. Or so they say. I've never had a car accident.

I see the grey car from in front parked by the roadside. Where is the car which hit me? Goodness. It must be that one. I'm surprised it was able to pull over. A front like that – all folded and, well… *mashed.* Fear creeps down my throat. I swallow. I haven't even checked my own car.

It's even worse.

The back is bent up like a crinkled chip. The boot door is ajar. I push down. It bounces back up. I move back to the bonnet. My poor, poor car. You were once so *car-shaped*. Now you look like a can someone used to play street soccer. Mercilessly.

How am I going to get to the hospital?

I need photos. Details. Number plates. A sheet of calmness falls over me. I'm not injured. Thank you, Lord. *I can do this*. I walk towards the grey car. One step at a time.

'Hi!'

'Hey.' The windows are down. There's an old, Italian-looking couple inside.

'What happened?' The man leans out, arm draped over the window sill. Grey moustache. Grizzled hair.

'The car behind crashed into me. I got pushed into you.'

'That woman?' He twists to point behind and then begins talking to his wife in urgent undertones. I look over my shoulder and see a white woman pacing by the side of the road near the smashed car. She's on her phone.

'I think so.'

The Italian man opens his door. 'Look, there's barely a scratch on our car. We'll get her insurer and clear off. We've got somewhere to be.'

So do I. I should ring Jasmine to tell her I'm going to be late. How late? Can I even drive my car the rest of the way? We're only fifteen minutes from the hospital. No. I can't ring her. She'll be upset. 'Okay, sure.'

The other driver is still on her phone, too far away to hear us. He scowls in her direction. 'She must have come flying 'round the roundabout, and not realised we were all banked up. I'm going to talk to her.'

I watch as he walks up, phone in hand. She ends her call. They speak and gesture and type on their phones. The man returns. His wife is craning her neck out the car door. 'We're going.' He pauses. 'Should get your rego.'

'Oh. Um.' What is it? I must look like an idiot. 'Sorry, I've only had the car three months. I'll have to check—'

'Don't worry, I'll just take a picture.' He snaps my poor battered car with his phone. 'You alright?'

'Yeah.'

They drive away. *Am* I alright? I guess I have to be. 'Excuse me!' I walk to where the woman is still gripping her phone like a lifeline. 'We should – er...' Turn back time? Pretend nothing happened? '...exchange details?'

She jerks around. Dark hair. A smart sort of jacket. Sunglasses. Most importantly, middle-aged. An adult. *Finally*, someone to tell me what comes next. 'I don't know what happened!' she wails. 'I was just driving and then, I don't know what happened!'

I do. 'You – er – you drove into my car. And I got pushed into the other car. The grey one.'

'I was on my way to the hospital!' She's crying. 'I had an appointment and I was so stressed and now this happens!'

'Um... I was going to the hospital too.' Am I comforting or informing? A bit of both. 'My sister's in the Children's.'

'*Oh!*' She shatters into fresh tears. 'Oh that's worse! I don't know what happened. I just don't know...'

'I'm sorry.' I give up hope that she'll be the one taking charge. Suddenly it doesn't matter. She looks so desolate. So... *helpless*. 'It's going to be okay.' I step forward and give her a light hug. 'It's okay.' Please stop crying. 'It's not your fault – er... Well, er, it is actually.' I pat her microfibre shoulder. 'But it could happen to anyone, it's easy to do.' I pull away.

'Thank you, oh sweetie. Sorry. I should be...,' she sniffs. 'I should be hugging you!'

'It's okay.' I repeat. Please believe me. I smile. 'Um… can I pray for you?' It's all I have to offer. I close my eyes before she can reply. 'Dear Lord, thank you for keeping us safe and please help, er… everything else to go smoothly. Please be our comfort and be with us. Amen.'

'Bless you! Bless you!' She's crying again.

'I'm Emily, by the way.'

Her phone trills. 'It's my insurance company.' She puts it to her ear. I step aside. Should I be doing the same? Do I even have my insurance number? It *might* be in my glove-box.

'Oi! Is this yer car?' A stringy man lopes towards me. Where did he come from? And where did that huge tow truck come from? 'Do yer need to be towed?'

'Um. I don't know.' An adult! But I don't trust him. Will he charge me? Oh Lord, what do I do? 'I think I should ring my insurance company.'

'Whose fault was it?'

'Hers.' I gesture at the microfibre woman, preoccupied with her call.

'Then yer fine.' His singlet hangs off his muscular brown shoulders. 'If yer jump in the cab of m'truck I can take yer to a hire car place.'

I'm tempted. It would be so easy to follow his lead. But no, I can do this. Still that peace. That calmness. I breathe in. 'I need to make some phone-calls first.' And take some pictures. What if someone blames me for this mess?

The office is small and crowded. Ledgers overflow with paper, and car manuals are stacked by the wall. It smells of oil and car fresheners and soggy plastic. The last one is my fault. Bags of once-fresh produce mill at my ankles and sweat. My oil-streaked stool is far too high and broken as well. I skim the toes of my sandals on the concrete floor.

'We're just cleaning the hire car and then it's all yours, love.' The middle-aged receptionist types faster, her fake nails clacking against the keyboard. 'Just some details: what suburb was the accident in?'

'Er… near a roundabout? And a bridge?'

She smiles and pushes her gum back with her tongue. 'I'll check where our driver picked you up.'

'Thanks.' I stare around as she continues the paperwork. A silver industrial fan struggles against the heat. I don't feel anything. That's good. I can't afford to feel, not yet… If she takes much longer I'm going to start feeling, violently. Poor Jay. She'll think I slept in. How much longer are they going to be? It's so hot in here. I want a shower. Everything aches.

'Here we go love, our hire car man is coming and he'll get a signature and give you the key.'

'Thanks.' I don't want a key. I never want a key again. Or a car. If I have to get inside another car, and a strange car at that, I think I'll throw up. Someone will hit me again. The roads aren't safe. I can't risk it. I can't die – what will Jasmine do? I won't drive. I *won't*.

'Hello. Emily is it? Greg.' My hand feels like a swimming pool against his. 'Let's talk about the hire car, shall we?'

'Yes, thank you.' Without a car I will be stranded in this stuffy office forever. I need a car for Jasmine. I need to drive for Jasmine. *Oh Lord, don't let me crash.*

Euphoria. I deflate against the cool plastic and gaze at Jasmine, soaking her in. I made it. I'm alive. *I drove.*

'There you are! Mum messaged to say you'd be late…'

'I had an accident. A car drove into mine and I had to be towed and get a hire car and the insurance company was confusing and I hope I've done the right thing—'

'What? Are you okay? Are you hurt?'

'I'm fine! I'm fine. It wasn't that big. Nothing major… goodness, I'm hot. I'm so hot.' All at once I'm suffocating. 'I think I'm going to melt. I need water. I need—'

'A fan?' Jasmine hands me a paper fan shaped like a small paddle.

Oh brilliant! Oh delight of delights! I beat the stifling air towards me. '*Ahh.*' I wish I could get my legs to relax. My calf muscles are bunched so tightly they hurt. My hands are shaking. Why? It's all over.

Except it's not. The hire car has ants, and shakes and rattles and I'm too short to see over the steering wheel properly and it's so hot out there it feels like the world's melting into cement coloured puddles and... 'Where on *earth* did you get this fan?'

Jay smirks. 'It's AIDS Day; didn't you see the posters? They're handing out freebies all over the place.'

I look down at the piece of cardboard in my hand. *Test more. Treat early. Stay safe.* ENDING HIV.

Saved by a virus. I break into giggles.

Courage brother, do not stumble,
though thy path be dark as night.

I can't stop crying. It's 10 pm and thirty degrees and I'm spread cross-eagle on my bedroom carpet with an old orange hymn book. I cry for my car and the month it'll take to fix it. I cry because sometimes the last straw is exactly that, the last straw.

There's a star to guide the humble,
trust in God and do the right.

I cry for Jasmine because there's no end in sight. I cry because bad things aren't coming in threes but in three-hundreds and I just want them to stop.

Let the road be rough and dreary
and its end far out of sight.

I cry because this suffocating summer won't end and it's too hot to breathe. I cry because everyone else is celebrating graduation and lazing at the beach and I feel so alone.

Foot it bravely; strong or weary,
Trust in God and do the right.

I cry and I read. I read and I cry. *Please Lord, what good are you summoning out of this?* Why does life have to hurt so much? *Courage brother, courage* breathes the warm night. *Courage, trust in God.*

I don't know how much courage I have left.

DIARY EXCERPTS
December 3 – 12, 2015

Misty-rain and feeling grumbly
(79 days in hospital)
Oh Lord, please bring Jas home. Please. Please, take me. Help me to glorify Your Name in all of this.

Waiting for the happy ending
(80 days in hospital)
…victory is always assured, because the Lord is righteous. But it may not come straight away. There may be many furrows. Many furrows but no victory… please help me to cling to that. Especially now, when the days stretch on and on.

One star in the darkness
(82 days in hospital)
Today was nice…Spent the day with Jay in the hospital. Convinced her to do schoolwork, chatted, coloured and ate her dessert. It was hot again.

My greatest fear
(85 days in hospital)
...That's our fear, isn't it? That all our suffering would be for nothing. That there will be no purpose and no reward.

Is anything about to begin?
(87 days in hospital)
Again I wake up late. Again Mum is unwell. Again the school is hard to contact [re: Jasmine's HSC]. The saga never ends.

Facing fearful odds
(89 days post admission)
At the risk of sounding repetitive: I'm very tired… We are still waiting with Jasmine. It's in God's hands. I just can't comprehend another disappointment. Humanly, the odds are not in our favour. But they are. They always are, whatever the outcome.

Chapter Twenty-five: Picking Up the Pieces

'Turn it down. Quick!'

'Relax, it doesn't last long.'

'Emily! Turn the volume *down!*'

'It's only a *few* swear words.' Goodness, is she three years old? I can't find the volume button. 'We're in a hospital, not a police station.'

'Exactly!' Her fingers push mine away, fumbling for the mute button. 'A *children's* hospital!'

Ah, good point. All those innocent ears. 'One sec... oh look! It's over now.'

Jay sighs.

'Ooh this is scary! Is he going to drown?'

'Not telling. Just watch.'

'He's going to drown, isn't he? I can always tell!'

'Yeah, like how you can "always" predict the exact time a car trip will take?'

'I can! It's not my fault people drive slowly.'

'Listen! This is a good quote.' I snuggle closer and squint at the laptop screen. 'It's my favourite part.'

"You want to know how I did it?..." A panting, bare-chested, spindle-legged man yells at his taller, athletic brother on the shore of the beach. *"This is how I did it: I never saved anything for the swim back."*

'See!' I lean back on Jasmine's pillow. 'You can definitely use that quote for the first module. He discovers the only way to achieve his goal is to give his all. Everything... Jay?' I nudge her shoulder with mine. 'Are you listening – oh, watch out! Don't move your knee—'

The laptop tilts out of view. 'Quick! Catch it! Why did you move?'

'I wouldn't have moved if you hadn't moved the bed!'

'I didn't move the bed! I moved *me*...'

'... which moved the bed.'

I pull the hospital laptop back onto the white sheets. 'We'll have to rewind. There was a good film technique in that scene as well...'

Jasmine lies back down. Where's the re-wind button? 'So, are you going to?' I ask.

She wiggles, her body warm against mine. 'Huh?'

I roll my eyes. 'Are you going to use this for a related text? I still have all my notes, and my topic isn't *that* different from yours…'

'Maybe.' Her lips curve. It's a yes.

'Brilliant. One text, two to go! We're practically half way there.'

'Emily, we haven't even finished the movie yet.'

'I'm not going to talk.'

'Okay.'

'I've got nothing to say.'

'Okay.'

'I'm sick of complaining about the traffic. We should have an afternoon nap.'

Jay sighs. 'I'm trying.'

'Here we go!'

'Ooh.' Jay stares at the two mini gelato cones. 'I thought they might be all gone.'

'Nope, there were lots. I got you pink.' I perch on the end of her bed and deposit a handful of serviettes on the blanket.

'Mmm.'

'Yeah. It's a pity you can't go outside, it's the right weather for eating gelato.'

'I never realised you got so many freebies in hospital!'

'It's 'cause it's a children's hospital. Everyone feels bad. You know… all those poor sick kids in hospital over Christmas.'

'True.' The tip of Jay's tongue runs over the pink gelato with surgical precision.

'We haven't put the Christmas tree up at home.'

She shrugs. 'So?'

'We'll do it together when you're discharged.'

'Mmm.'

I wince. There it is again. Every time I mention the future her voice changes, as if she's traded her humanity for something mechanical.

'Jay…'

'They're going to take my drain out tomorrow.'

Is she trying to sound unconcerned? What a joke. As if either of us could be blasé about this. A drain removal is the moment of truth, the pouring of iron into a crucible. 'Finally.' I bite into my waffle cone. 'Urgh, it's soft.'

'Do you think I'll leak?'

So tentative. What am I? Psychic? The Oracle of Delphi? I sigh and wrap my half-eaten cone in a serviette. 'I dunno, Jay. I really hope not.'

'Me too.'

'Jay…' I suddenly feel compelled to prepare her for the worst. No one else will. 'Jay… even if you're not home for Christmas… we'll celebrate after, okay?'

No response.

'I really, really hope God's plan is to bring you home.' I slip my shoes off so I can curl up at the foot of her bed. 'But if it's not… well, he's still with you, you know?'

Still no response. She's blinking. 'You know?' I repeat.

'I know.' It's quiet, scarcely more than a breath. Yet it's not the sound of a robot, but a living human being.

I meet Mum in the corridor. 'She says she's fat,' I whisper. 'She won't eat her sandwich.'

I've read of people appearing 'pained'. Now I know what it looks like. Mum glances at the door to Jasmine's ward and back again. 'They weighed her yesterday. She's put on seven kilos.'

'No wonder!' I fight to keep my voice down. I'm scared. 'She hasn't walked in two months. There's nothing for her to do all day and meals mark the time.'

'I know. It's the cortisone as well. She's been on such high doses…' Mum shakes her head. 'I'm just saying I can understand how she feels. She doesn't want to be fat.'

'She's not fat.' I grind.

'No,' Mum amends, 'but she is a bit… chubby.'

'She's refusing her lunch.'

'I know,' Mum says, 'that's silly. I'll go talk to her.'

We enter together. Jay looks at us suspiciously. 'Were you talking about me?'

'Yes.' Mum sits down. Always the direct approach. 'Emily said you don't want your sandwich.'

'I'm fat.'

'How can you be? All your fat is up your nose, stopping that leak.' I grin. It's an old joke. She doesn't smile.

Instead of pity I feel a splinter of pleasure. I fight myself as Mum encourages and cajoles and generally dispenses no-nonsense common sense. For the first time in a decade I am comfortable in my body and Jay is not.

By the time she was three years old she refused to wear pants because they were ugly. She'd wage battles before church. *'It's the middle of winter, Jasmine.' 'I want to wear a dress!'* By the time I was twelve I was thoroughly sick of long hair and lopped it off at my earlobes. I'd wanted to be a boy for as long as I could remember, it just seemed *easier*.

Books led me to believe that teenage girls enjoy becoming women. I hated it with a vehement passion. All of a sudden I had curves everywhere. Curves that made running and sleeping on my stomach difficult. Curves that mean all my old clothes did not fit and all my new ones made me feel awkward. Then there were pimples. By sheer force of will I told myself I didn't care... but they hurt all the same.

Meanwhile, Jasmine remained lithe and beautiful. Compared to her I was a lumbering woman-child with lank hair. I refused to allow myself to be jealous – that was weak and cowardly – but if I had, I would have been jealous of her dimples and her curly light brown hair and her photogenic smile.

I've never hated my body but it's taken a decade to feel comfortable in it. Ten years to come home. I've lost weight over the last ten weeks as surely as Jasmine has gained it. My personal cocktail was one of stress and busyness and simply not caring. I don't feel stocky anymore and three years after the end of my teen years my skin is finally clear. My hair is growing back thick and healthy and finally dipping below my earlobes. The past months have birthed a steady confidence, the type one gets from loving and defending another person.

These days I not only feel comfortable. I sometimes feel pretty.

And Jasmine? In contrast, Jasmine is the one who has become uncomfortable and awkward in her body. Five years too late and under the influence of artificial hormones Jasmine at last knows how it feels. Shame sweeps through me. I can't look at her. 'I'm heading off.' A kiss to Jay, a hug to Mum. 'I love you,' I say.

I just don't feel as sad for you as I should.

I flee to my hire car. Shoving the sun-shield off the windscreen, I clamp my palms down on the burning steering wheel. Turning up my audio of *Paradise Lost* to almost shouting level, I reverse and join the line of waiting cars at the intersection.

"What can escape the eye of God all-seeing, or deceive his heart omniscient?" It's only fair she should know the peculiar pain of feeling ugly, I argue. I don't *really* feel *happy* about her struggle.

"Man... with strength entire, and free will... manifold in sin, deserved to fall." I cut Mr. Milton off with a furious stab, and cross over two lanes, trying to both ignore and excuse my shame in the sudden silence. But as I creep out from the airport tunnel my self-delusion shatters. I see my heart as starkly as the brake lights of the car in front. It's not a nice sight.

Sitting on hard, plastic chairs doesn't make you a saint anymore than brain tumours do. The tally of hours you spend at a hospital doesn't edge you any closer to selflessness. Illness doesn't strip away spite or vanity. I wish it did. Despite the enormity of the situation, and the sacredness of the term 'brain tumour' I'm really just an ordinary, broken person, muddling along, stabbing innocent bystanders with my flaws and petty jealousies, overlooking grace.

I sigh as the traffic stalls, and flip the audio book back on. *'Whom shall [God] send...? Whom but thee...Son... Man's Friend, his Mediator... both Ransom and Redeemer.'*

And right there is the hope in my brokenness. Thanks, Mr. Milton.

Chapter Twenty-six: I'll Give You Anything

Something's not right. I snap open my eyes. What is it? I roll over in bed. My stomach flip-flops like a dead fish.

Urgh. The dead fish begins making bubbly noises as if it's trying to stage a resurrection. Quick! Out of bed. Open door. Bathroom. Need bathroom –

Just in time. I double over on the toilet. My stomach spits and hisses. The fish wins first prize for persistence. Sweat breaks out like goose pimples over my back. What did I eat for dinner last night? My tongue feels like shrivelled orange peel. I stumble downstairs. Glass. Water. Sip. That's better. All better – *Urgh.* Bathroom – bathroom! Who closed the door? Who put down the lid?

Oh *fiddlesticks*. The fish groans. So do I. My forehead bumps against my knees. I don't think I'm going anywhere further than a ten second sprint from the toilet today.

Today. Oh no. I'm supposed to visit the Super Close Hospital today. The one everyone's praying I'll get a job at. The one which doesn't have a vacant position but said I could drop around…

I can just imagine the phone call. 'Yeah sorry, I really wanted to come but I've got a fish in my tummy and it wants out.' Sounds legitimate.

The shower's running upstairs. Mum must be well enough to visit Jay. I spread fingers through my bed hair. I feel awful. I leave a message on the Super Close Hospital's answering machine and stumble to the lounge-room. Blanket. Water. Panadol. *Braveheart* DVD.

The fish and I sign out.

'I want a home and children and peace… But it's all for nothing if I don't have freedom!'

Derr. Derr. Derr. I whimper. I don't want to speak to anyone. Was Mum expecting a call? I hit pause. *Sorry, William Wallace.* I agree with you: freedom sounds lovely, and so does peace. 'Hello-this-is-Emily.'

There's a silence. I wait for an indication that I can hang up. 'Good morning. I'm ringing from the Nepean Blue Mountains Local Health District. The purpose of my call is to inform you that if you are still available we'd like to offer you a full time position as a Radiographer Level 1…'

I put the phone down and burst into tears. Confusion and sickness vie for my attention. I think I just got a job. From an interview I thought I failed weeks and weeks ago.

This was the only hospital which is distant enough for me to move out – freedom, independence, adventure – and close enough so I can return whenever I'm needed. This was the only hospital which can be classified as both rural and urban. This was the only hospital which was exactly what I wanted. *Impossible.*

I cry harder. You answered my prayer, Lord! There was no chance of getting a rural hospital close enough to support Jasmine... but I got one. *I have a job!* No more applications. No more chasing up interviews. No more visiting employment agencies. Freedom! Oh William Wallace, I'm with you all the way! For Scotland and Radiography! For—

Urgh. My fish cartwheels, and I sprint to the toilet.

I wander into Mum and Dad's room and sit on the worn carpet in front of the balcony. Arms around my knees, I stare off into the distance. I'm still in shock. I know I shouldn't be. I know God can do impossible things and answer impossible prayers. But to answer this one, to give me the job I want...

I shake my head. Why did you do it, Lord? It wasn't that important. Not really. Not in the grand scheme of things. Not as important as Jasmine. Nothing hinged on it. Not really. Job satisfaction isn't a human necessity.

I smile at the huge gum tree outside the window. Its thousands of leaves are bending over in the hot wind, like a blurry shoal of tadpoles. What would it be like to swim in the middle of a shoal like that? You'd feel so surrounded, so supported, so loved.

Exactly as I feel right now. You did this for me, Lord? Just for me? I let myself fall back onto the scratchy carpet. I really should vacuum soon. *You did the impossible for me!* I beam at the ceiling. It doesn't mind. This house hasn't seen a proper smile for far too long. *You listened to my shower prayer. You answered.*

Should I… no. But why not? *Why ever not?* I'm going to pray another impossible prayer, Lord. I could tackle a lion right now. But I can't heal Jasmine. You can. Please heal her. Bring her home. Let her be discharged on… it's the fourteenth of December today. Christmas is in two weeks… it would be nice if she was home a few days beforehand to get settled …the twenty-second of December.

Dear Lord, please bring Jasmine home on the twenty-second of December. I'm going to pray this every day. Please, in your mercy listen. You've given me a job. Now give me back my sister.

I fumble through my handbag, stomach seizing with familiar cramps. These are not caused by sickness. 'I'm going to the toilet.' Why didn't I remember to wear something with pockets?

'You just went,' Jay mumbles, half asleep. I don't answer, but when I reach the ward door I turn. Her eyes are closed and she's breathing deeply. She looks tiny.

As a child she loved playing dolls. Now at least once a year she tells me the names she's picked out for her children. I greet them with a snort and a raised eyebrow. It's our ritual.

It must be difficult to have children without a pituitary gland. The pamphlets haven't been particularly detailed about this. Dad visits Jay every night after work, but on the rare times when we're all at home we swap news of our hospital shifts and scour them together, searching for answers to the questions we're too afraid to ask. I wanted to design coasters when I grew up. Jay wanted to be a mum.

The future is impenetrable. Everything depends on how Jay is in the next hour, how the next surgery goes, what news the next doctor brings. We're living in stasis, and it is exhausting. Human beings, I suspect, are made to plan and dream. But how can we? We don't know what will remain after all this is over. If it's ever over.

I stare at my sister's sleeping face, relaxed, unpained, unsuspecting. A hot, alien, tightness rises in my chest. It's sacrificial and possessive, it's violent and yet extremely rational. It's fierce, and when it speaks, it says: *I'll stand beside you. I won't leave.*

My fists are clenched, and my eyes ache from the intensity of the moment. Whatever you need me from me, you can have. Whatever you need me to do, I'll do. I swear.

You just have to ask.

A woman enters the four bed ward. She's not wearing scrubs. I don't recognise her as a parent. Who has she come to visit? She beelines towards Jasmine. *Us.*

I stand up to intercept, finger on my lips. 'She's asleep.' Then I remember. Today the Lady-Who-Will-Teach-Us-Jay's-Emergency-Stress-Drug is coming. 'I'm Emily. Sister. Mum couldn't be here, but if you show me I can teach her.'

She looks me up and down. 'Is Jasmine your older sister?'

'Younger.'

She turns away from Jasmine's bed. 'There's a room down the corridor. We'll go there.' As I expect she leads me to the common room. What a life it has: party hall, church and now classroom. We drag two chairs out of the jumble and set them up facing each other. I sit straight, and smooth my skirt over my knees. Younger sister indeed.

'There's a video online,' she begins, 'in case you can't remember.'

I watch intently. There's a lot of fiddly steps. Pull the top off the vial. Attach the blunt needle to the syringe. Draw up the cortisol. Swap the blunt needle for the sharp one. I concentrate as if my own life depends on it, because one day, my sister's might.

'Now we practise injecting.' She draws out her *pièce de résistance* – a cream coloured pad which is apparently supposed to resemble a human thigh. 'You want to go into the muscle so you're going to have to use force.'

Force. I can do force. She places the pad on my skirt covered knee. 'The slower you do it, the more it will hurt.' Swift. I can be swift. 'Then again, she is most likely to be unconscious or at least immobile.'

Charming. I pick up the filled syringe. I can't afford to hesitate. Not now, if I am to prove myself to this woman or be useful to my parents. Not ever, if I want my sister to live. She nods her manicured eyebrows. 'Go ahead.'

I plunge the pen into the pad. There's a delay and then water floods across my thighs. Cold seeps into my skirts. I jump. Have I, surely not... A wet trail trickles down my knee and drips to the floor.

It's coming from the tan pad. *Phew.* I paste a nonchalant expression on my face and look up at the educator. I'm soaking wet.

'Well,' she says, 'well.'

'Was that right?'

'That was a bit *too* much force.' She draws her eyebrows back to their original position.

I push the pad onto the table and surreptitiously peel my saturated skirt from my legs. Why on earth isn't there a bag attached to the practice pad? Or is an impromptu shower part of the experience?

She clears her throat. 'Next time, less...*stabbing.*' She shapes the word like it's personally done her wrong. 'You don't want to strike her bone and leave behind broken bits of needle.'

Yes, that *does* sound like something to avoid. 'But apart from that?' I search for the bright side. 'Giving the dose is the most important thing, isn't it?'

She looks at me. 'Just remember: Next time, less *stabbing.*'

I pray to God there won't be a next time.

DIARY EXCERPTS
December 17 - 21, 2015

Dreaming of disaster
(94 days in hospital)

I woke at 4 am this morning with a bad dream and it took me a while to fall back asleep… I dreamt I was trapped in a car in the dark and no one was around and a man had reached a hand through the window and was pressing me down. Try as I might, nothing would give and I could not move an inch…

… I know you are the One above all who I can turn to… But Lord, suffering happens.

… I would rather you hear and say 'wait' than anyone else hear and rescue. I think. But it is terrifying. Oh may the day come when your 'wait' is 'now'! That you work through the deepest, darkest moments is brilliant. But that you are there, present … is a relief.

It goes on
(95 days in hospital)
… I can't sleep at night.

The veneer wears thin
(96 days in hospital)
Do I comment on sleep each time I'm here? Suffice to say I woke in the middle of the night… and am TIRED.

The day before the 22nd of December
(98 days in hospital)
Today I would have given up.
Some days, for no apparent reason, everything just becomes too much. Too much. For too long. In one sense it's silly and in another it's not. On one hand you feel like punching someone, on the other you're one blink away from bursting into tears. It's sort of frightening and childish… is this really how close I am to just losing it?

Is this all it takes, one unassuming day with its normal share of reliefs and sorrows?

Sometimes, yes. Apparently I won't receive my car back before Christmas. Apparently things don't get better when you think they should. Apparently when you're so close to the end, that's when your soul decides to give up. Thank God I had no life or death decisions to make…

If I were in a war or about to be tortured or had to rescue anyone: I would have simply given up today, and cried. And that would have been pathetic. Yet how many people does that happen to? How many deaths and tragedies are not actually representative of the life lived?

Chapter Twenty-Seven: The Twenty-Second of December

It's the twenty-second of December. The date means nothing to anyone else, but to me it means the world. I can hear someone on the phone downstairs. I check the time. Mum. Dad's left for work. I've slept in. There's only one person who would ring at this hour. Or rather, one place. Have you answered my prayer, God? Is Jasmine coming home?

I grab my dressing gown and make my way downstairs. Tread, pause. Tread, pause. I don't want to miss too much of the one-sided conversation.

'Okay, well that's good.'

Tread, pause.

'Me. I've only got a bit of a headache because my blood sugars weren't as low overnight, so I'll leave as soon as I have a shower.'

Tread, pause.

'I'll be as quick as I can.'

I reach the bottom of the steps.

'I love you too, Jasmine. I love you a lot.' Pause. 'Okay, bye.'

'Is she coming home?'

Mum turns, phone still in hand. 'That was Jasmine. I spoke to the nurse first and then her—'

'And?' I make a rolling motion with both hands.

'No, it doesn't sound like it. Endocrine hasn't given the 'all clear'. Might be a few more days. We have to pray it's before Christmas. Jasmine was a bit upset on the phone.'

Before Christmas? Upset? *I'm* upset! And far more than 'a bit'.

'Are you okay?' Mum comes over to the foot of the stairs.

No! No no no – 'Yeah.' A deep breath. 'I thought Jasmine might come home today.' I prayed and I prayed and I prayed and I—

Mum shrugs and grabs the banister. 'We can pray it won't be much longer than another week. There's still so much to sort out, I never thought it would be today.'

I did. I really did.

'I'm going to have a shower,' Mum says.

I move aside so she can go up the stairs. I can't cry yet. 'Are you sure you should go in?' I call after her.

'You've been so tired lately. I can go.' My voice wobbles and I wince. At least she can't see my face.

'No!' Mum's reply wafts down the staircase. 'I want to go. She wants me. I'm sure I'll feel a lot better after a shower.'

Once the blunt roar of water begins I dissolve in relief on the carpeted stairs. It's bad enough God has ignored my plea. To share a hospital room with the proof of His failure would be unendurable. Sobs roll up from my stomach and I hack them out like fur balls. I'm so disappointed. I'm so sad. I'm so *lost*.

The future fractures into puzzle pieces and I can't see how they will ever fit together again. I flounder up the stairs on my hands and knees. Crawling into my parents' bedroom I drag myself over to the glass balcony door. I stare at the huge gum-tree and its billions of leaves, swimming in sync with each warm gust. I'm back in the place where I first prayed my impossible prayer; what did I do wrong?

The shower will muffle any noise I make and I'm tired of crying quietly. My face is burning and heat floods across my chest. It's not anger. I'm too disappointed for anger. I brace my fingers against the raggedy white carpet and choke.

The shower switches off. I wipe my eyes and move to sit on the queen bed, drawing my dressing gown tight. I haven't tried to rub away my tears so I know I won't look blotchy. Just pink and tired.

'Oh!' Mum clutches her towel to her chest. I turn my back and fix my eyes on the hulking tree. 'What are you doing in here?'

I shrug obviously enough that she can read it from behind. 'Sitting. How's your headache?'

A sigh. I hear her getting dressed, throwing her towel down, slipping into trousers, muttering as her insulin pump gets tangled. 'Worse.'

'No good.' I should say more. But what? It's as if all the useful debris of everyday conversation has been vacuumed straight out of my head. It's my own fault. Hope is a thing with feathers and I *know* what happened to Icarus. Yet when God answered my first impossible prayer, I guess I thought...

'Jasmine sounded so upset – but I don't know if I can drive like this.' I hear the swish-swish of a vial being shaken. Eye drops or insulin? 'I thought my migraine would get better. Maybe in a few hours...'

I take a breath. It's like slurping cement. 'I'll go.'

'Are you sure? I really want to go, maybe in the afternoon...'

'It's fine.' The gum-leaves swell and crash in a bottle-green tidal wave. Each leaf spins out of control, caught in the mass movement of the trunk in the wind. To be one of them would be terrifying. 'I want to go,' I lie. It's harder than pulling a green branch off a healthy eucalypt. 'I really do.' I swivel away from the glass balcony doors. 'I'll give her a hug from you. I'll cheer her up.'

Mum frowns.

Sap bleeding, I smile.

I circle the hospital for the third time. The traffic is terrible today. It's been two hours since Mum spoke to Jay on the phone. I hope she's feeling calmer. I don't know how uplifting my presence is going to be.

Perhaps it was all a misunderstanding. Perhaps the nurse made a mistake. Perhaps Mum mis-heard. Perhaps God *will* bring Jasmine home today. You never know… Except I *do*. I'm trying to sew little pockets of fantasy to tuck my pain into. But I can't. I have to accept reality: Jay might not make it home before Christmas.

I read once that you can suppress feelings by conjuring a mental safe-box and locking them inside. Sure, it doesn't sound like the healthiest coping mechanism available, but if it's only for a short time… I only need six hours. Six hours to give Jay. Six hours of functionality and usefulness.

Surely I can do that…

Car parked. Phone checked. Disappointment and Grief and most importantly Hope folded away in a metallic green-blue box. I'm all set.

'Hey! It's me!'

'Emily!' Jay holds out her hands and I step into them. I give her a tight squeeze. It's not weird anymore. It's not even novel. 'I thought Mum was coming?'

'She was, but her headache is worse.' I drag up a smirk, 'You're going to have to put up with me instead.'

'O-kay.' Her smile teeters among her tear tracks.

'It's like a ghost-town in here!' I kick my bags beneath the plastic chair. 'Where is everyone?'

'Gone home.' Jay rubs her nose. 'Except for the girl next door. She's leaving this afternoon.' You'd expect an empty ward to be peaceful, a relief from the constant bustle. Instead it's eerie. Too quiet. A bit depressing. Or is that just because we're the ones left behind? 'Can I have some juice?'

'Yep.' I take my time, hunting methodically through the tiny fridge for a juice carton tagged with her ID sticker. I make myself a styrofoam cup of coffee and fill another with the ice I know Jay will ask for next. I pull out a carton of sticky date pudding in custard and check the best-before date. Will she want it? I'm not sure, but I stick it under my arm anyway in an attempt to minimise my back-

and-forth trips for the next thirty minutes. It's so hard to move this morning. 'Here you go Jay, and I found this—'

'Hello!' The nurse turns around and grins. Obs time already?

'Hi!' I juggle the three cups and make a beeline for the rolling table.

'Emily, I was just talking to Jasmine about the possibility of discharge today—'

'*What?*' I drop my cargo on the table. 'I mean, sorry. The hospital rang this morning, I thought...' It's a lie. It's a trick. *Retreat!* Don't listen, and above all, *don't* open the metal box of Hope.

'We've finally managed to contact the Endocrine Team. They're happy for discharge as long as the pharmacy is able to provide you with hormone replacements and pain relief until...'

I look at Jay. Her face is smeared with *ecstatic-terrified-unbelieving-cautious-happy*. Tinsel and candy-cane cut-outs dangle above her head, orphans of the Christmas Spirit which has been trampling determinedly through the wards since November.

'...of course we also need signatures from all your teams before we can discharge you.'

'Home?' Jay whispers. 'Today?' Is the nurse disturbed by our twin stares? One pair of eyes light, almost hazel. The other dark, blending to black. They are identical caches of hope and fear. The nurse doesn't know it, but this unity is almost as miraculous as the date: December twenty-second.

Home? Today?

'Looks like it!' The nurse chirps, and then sweeps out, seemingly unworried and entirely unaware of our nervousness. Do they have a subject on that at university? How to Remain Calm in the Presence of Absolutely Terrified Patients and their Family Members? She deserves a High Distinction.

'Eeek.' I deflate into a chair.

'Eeek,' Jay echoes in utter earnestness.

'Do you think...?'

'Will I really...?'

We've learnt not to give the future words, and it's a difficult habit to break. 'Eeek.' I say again. 'Should I ring Mum?'

'No!'

By her tone, I may as well have suggested we cancel Christmas.

'...Just in case.'

'Yeah. Good idea.' I put my phone down. 'Just in case.'

The greeny-blue Hope box bulges. I shove it away. She could begin leaking again any minute. One of her many specialist teams might refuse discharge. And if neither of these, well, her bed could collapse from the sheer weight of tense expectation and send her back to theatre with a broken leg.

It's possible. Hope may have feathers, but we don't all get to fly.

'I Spy?'

'No.'

'Ermm... I could read something?' I slump in the bedside chair and squint at the Christmas decorations. The tinsel and cut-outs explode into supernovas, like when I drive at night without my glasses. It's easier to forget the ward is empty this way.

Jay giggles.

'What's so funny?' I lug open my eyelids.

'Me!' She tilts her phone. It's in selfie-mode and the angle offers her four double chins. I roll my eyes and pull my jacket tighter around my neck. It's cold in here. I suppose there's no one except us to suck up the air-con. The girl next door left an hour ago in a whirlwind of parents and siblings and balloons.

Rain slides down the windows like sheets of newly minted coins. The relentless beat reverberates through the ward, unimpeded by the usual cacophony of people and machines. I shiver.

'Smile!'

I stick out my tongue, eyes closed. Waiting is exhausting.

'C'mon!'

I smile. I like this Jasmine. Silly and confident and seventeen-going-on-twelve. Much better than angel-look-alike Jasmine or wraith-pale Jasmine or cynical-tired Jasmine.

'Open your eyes.'

'No.' I pull my hood over my ears and curl my arms. In this position the plastic chair is almost survivable. 'I'm going to sleep. Wake me when they've discharged you.'

A giggle. There's a luxury to closing your eyes in company. It's an acknowledgement that enough is right with the world and your companions that you can afford to be less-than-capable for a while. I indulge. After all, it's the twenty-second of Dec- *no*. I don't dare. I can't open the box. Can't sprout feathers. It's still the eleventh hour and there's time enough for them to fall off.

A shuffling of blankets. 'You're taking photos of me, aren't you?' I don't open my eyes. She can capture me huddled-in-a-plastic-chair for all posterity if she likes (she does). Why shouldn't camera rolls be realistic?

'Hello!'

I almost fall out of the chair. Action all stations! Flipping back my hood I regain 240 degree vision. 'Oh!' I say, 'I didn't know you were coming!'

A mother and daughter, family friends. They smile from the foot of the bed. 'I messaged your mum,' the woman explains, 'and she said she'd let you know. We thought we'd drop in to see how things are going.'

Whoops. I imagine the phone log of missed messages and calls. It's what happens when you close your eyes for ten minutes in a hospital. 'Good to see you!' I stand up to make room. 'We're waiting for the teams to be contacted...' I look at Jay. She looks back. I sigh. We're supposed to at least fake hope. It's the rules. Otherwise visitors get depressed or *concerned*. '... she might be discharged today!'

'Oooh!' Jay's friend draws up a chair. 'How exciting!' The two girls launch into conversation punctuated with giggles and slightly hysterical laughter. The mother looks at me. Really looks. Can she read my fear? I suspect so. She's well acquainted with the hospital system herself. Her smile is so reassuring and comfortable-looking I might cry. Might, but won't. The lock on my metallic box holds fast.

'Discharge takes forever, doesn't it?' She glances at the girls. 'I might duck down for a coffee and they can chat for a while. Makes the time go quicker. Do you want anything?'

'No thanks.' I smile. 'I guess I'd better, er... better *pack*.' It becomes real. Jasmine is hopefully-probably-most-likely going home today. I look from the tinsel overhead, to the overflowing cupboard, to the cluttered bedside table.

I should probably get started.

'Hey Mum. How are you?'

'My headache is worse. I just took more meds. Is Jasmine okay?'

'Yeah.' I swallow. Breathe. In, out. 'They-said-she-can-come-home-today.'

'What? But what about all the medications? What about the Endocrine Team? You didn't push them did you? You know it's better that everything's sorted out than her to get home and have to be readmitted the next day—'

I whisk the phone from my ear. 'Mum! Stop!' I close my eyes. 'Can you at least sound happy? It *wasn't* my idea; *they* offered and *they* said it was okay. All her teams agree.'

'Okay,' Mum says. There's a pause. I move the phone back to my ear. Her voice comes again. 'But are you *sure* it's alright?'

No. I'm not sure. I'm not sure about anything except it's the twenty-second of December... '*Yes.* Yes, I'm sure. They're getting everything ready now.'

'Don't forget a discharge letter.' Always the voice of reason. 'Are you certain it's not too late? It's already 3 pm. Did you know it is absolutely *pouring* rain and—'

'It's going to happen!' I hang up.

'There. That's everything!'

The row of nurses smile. I swipe rain droplets from my hair. It's incredible how many trips it takes to move ninety-nine days worth of gifts and belongings to a car. I turn to Jay. 'Alright. So I parked in the pick-up zone so you just have to make it to the front door.' It took her fifteen minutes to get from the bed to the chair she's in now. She hasn't walked more than ten metres in three months. I have no idea how she is going to get down to the ground floor.

'Okay.' Jay grins. She is shining.

'Er, I have a question.' I move over to the nurses and lower my voice. 'What if her antidiuretic hormones run out while we're in the car? It can take us two hours to get home…'

'She's got a water bottle with her. And her tablets.'

'But what if she has to go to the toilet?'

'It will be fine.'

Will it? Will it really? How can I trust anything will be fine again after all the times in the past ninety-nine days when it wasn't? 'Are you sure?'

'You'll get home. It will be fine.' The nurses say together, the epitome of peace and good-will. 'All the best!' They hug Jay.

'Thank you for…' I wave at the forlorn Christmas decorations and the empty room. '…*everything.*'

'We're going to miss you both.'

I can't say the feeling's mutual, so I say nothing. We've been waiting three months to walk out this door.

The answer to the problem of reaching the car, it turns out, is Determination. Agonizing, limping, *whimpering* Determination. Determination punctured by pleas to give up and patched with stern dismissals. Jasmine collapses in the passenger seat. She's in tears. I close her door. Rain pulses down my neck. We're not going back.

'Sorry, Jay.' I flip on the windscreen wipers and turn the ignition. I can't hear the engine because my heart is thudding too loudly, so I twist the key again. The car scrapes and splutters. 'Jay, we need to pray.' I creep out of the hospital pick-up zone. 'We need to pray right now. Will you pray?'

She shakes her head. Tears are plopping off her cheekbones. Is she angry? Or overwhelmed? Or as terrified as me?

'Dear Lord, please be with us. Help us to get home safely, and thank you for letting Jay leave hospital today. We thank you so much. Amen.' Water smashes down onto my windscreen. I can only just see the car in front. Spray springs up from the bitumen in misty fountains as we wade through the lights of crawling vehicles.

God, don't let us die. Don't let me kill her. *Please* don't let me kill her. I ease my foot down on the accelerator. My arms are shaking. I'm thankful Jay's staring out the side window. I know Hope has feathers but so does the albatross, that mythical harbinger of doom. 'Let's sing!' I say.

Jay bursts into tears.

I long to do the same, but right now there's *more* than enough water in the universe. Jaw clenched, I drive on.

And on.

We turn into the driveway at home at last. It feels like a dream, and not just because of the rain and fog. This universe, the one where Jay comes home from hospital on the twenty-second of December, healed of a brain-tumour, can't be real. Miracles don't happen. I'm afraid to breathe too loudly in case something breaks and we're catapulted back to the hospital and reality.

Then Dad opens the door. 'She's home! The princess is home!'

'Daaad.'

And suddenly, with all the shock of two realities colliding, everything is real. So, so real. We struggle into the house, wet, sweaty and exhausted. We scatter plastic bags and sodden discharge papers and tears beside the shoe rack. We breathe through the anti-climax and the retreating adrenaline. Still, the key word is 'we'. The key word will *always* be 'we' from now on, when it comes to Jasmine and I.

There's no going back to the old world, and I don't want to. Hope is a thing with feathers, but my God cares about the smallest of sparrows, and tonight he brought one home.

Final

DIARY EXCERPT
December 22, 2015 (99 days in hospital; 1 day home)

An ending at last.
Jay is home.
Home.
Home.
HOME…Oh Lord. What can I say? You answer prayers. In the face of ALL odds You brought Jas home – today. Tuesday. The day I prayed for. Oh, praise be to You!

… *thank You.* Thank You for tonight.

Epilogue: Unexpected Answers
18 months later

'Mmm... so good.' The coffee trickles down my throat, a few degrees away from scalding. The perfect temperature.

'Yeah.'

I raise an eyebrow, feeling lazy. 'You haven't even touched yours.'

Jay peers at her plastic covered cup as though it's a red-bellied black snake and she's the furthest you can get from a reptile wrangler. Actually, she probably is. 'Is it hot?'

'Mmm hmm.' I smile at the disposable cup. You beautiful thing, you. A jogger passes by on our left. The bush huddles in dry clumps to our right. Our path meanders in front of us, threading through the park reserve with about as much energy as I have after my long drive this morning. None. 'It's a waste to let it go cold.'

'Hmmm.' Scepticism parades across Jay's face. She sticks her tongue into the little sip hole. 'Ow!'

'Silly! You need to pour it like this.' I take a swig. *Ah.* 'If you're ever afraid it's too hot, just pour a bit underneath your tongue instead of on top. You have no temperature receptors there.'

'Or I could just wait until it's cooler.' Jay clutches the huge cup in both hands. 'I feel so posh. Like a business woman in the city.'

I snort. Wandering through a scruffy park on Saturday morning, we are about as far as you can get from business women in the city. Still… 'Me too. I've never got a super sized coffee before.'

'Really?'

'No!' Contrary to popular belief, shift work does not always turn one into a coffee addict. 'A coffee this size is normally like seven dollars.' Another jogger passes us. 'This is pretty good for service station coffee.'

'Pity it's written on the bottom.'

'What?'

Jay tips her cup. '"Three dollars".'

'Oh.'

Jay sniggers. 'We're so posh.' She holds her cup normally. 'Whoops!' She tilts her cup to her mouth and flashes me the three dollar sign on the base. 'No we're not!' She turns the cup the right way again. 'Yes we are.' She tilts it. 'Whoops! No we're not—'

'Okay!' Happiness trembles over my shoulders this morning. Nothing can take it away, not even embarrassing coffee cups – or embarrassing sisters. How different this Jay is from the (literal and metaphorical) cripple who was discharged from hospital all those months ago. 'I'm so glad you're finally out of that boot.'

'Me too.' The depth Jay puts into those two words is one of sheer relief. 'I never, ever thought I'd get stress fractures from lying down for three months.'

I 'never, ever thought' my little sister would get a brain tumour, and look how that turned out.

'So how's work?'

'What? Oh.' I take a sip of coffee. Blah, it's getting cold. 'Good. Busy. My workmates are great. Living so far away though is… hard.' A mother with a pram overtakes us. 'I… I'm glad I'm not working this weekend.' Another jogger. He looks about eighty. He'd better not trip. I don't have my portable x-ray machine with me. 'I… I miss you.'

'I miss you too.' Jay drinks.

'How is uni going?'

'Good.' She looks sideways. 'Busy. I like anatomy and physiology best. Some of the other subjects I'm not exactly sure how they're going to help me with occupational therapy though.'

I smirk. 'Sounds like every uni course everywhere.'

'It's fun but tiring.'

'You do travel a lot.' We come out of the reserve and follow the path parallel to the main road. It's deserted this early on a weekend. 'How's the uni Christian group?'

'Alright.' Jay sips her coffee. 'I can't make any of the meetings 'cause of my lectures.'

'Oh.' I watch her lick the plastic top of her cup. 'And are you... are you reading anything in the Bible yourself?'

'Yeah.' She sucks foam off her lip. 'I'm trying to read through Isaiah, but it's a bit confusing.' She shrugs. 'I don't really get it.'

I keep walking. At least, my outer body keeps walking. The white pavement pushes back against the soles of my shoes. The wind rushes past. My coffee cools. Inside, however, I've frozen. My inner self is standing stock-still in a meadow surrounded by little yellow flowers. The type adults call weeds and every child knows are not. I'm not a very pretty statue, my mouth is hanging open.

'I've got a commentary on Isaiah. It's really good, more like a devotion book really...' My outer body waffles on; my inner self slowly becomes unstuck. 'That is, if you want... if you're... interested?'

'Yeah, sounds good.' Jay smiles. We walk on. My inner self tries to as well, but gets side-tracked tacking up a plaque among the yellow flowers: *First Non Awkward Conversation About Faith*.

I swallow. Lord, is it true? That prayer I prayed all those years ago: *Make her love you more than anything. Please. Whatever it takes…* are you answering that prayer now?

'I have a question.'

'Hmm… *What?*' My outer self and inner self collide. I drop my tools in the meadow and choke on my cold coffee. 'Sorry. Yes?'

Jasmine shuffles her cup in her hands. 'It's just, this is going to sound awful, but well…' She meets my eyes. 'Sometimes people complain about a headache or something small and I don't know what to do because I feel annoyed and I know I should sympathise with them but also it's such a tiny thing and they go on and on, and – what should I do?'

My inner self *and* my outer self freeze. 'You're… you're asking me?'

Jay nods. Her eyes meet mine and I've had far too much practice not to be able to take a stab at reading the expressions passing through them. Nervousness. Frustration… and something else. Trust. Absolute, unbridled *trust*.

I resist the urge to look behind me. To turn and try to find the person to whom Jasmine is baring her soul. The person she thinks has all the answers.

And I remember the second half of the prayer I prayed all those years ago. *She doesn't have to love me, Lord, we don't even have to get along. It will hurt, but she can hate me, just let her love you!*

This reciprocated love, this friendship between us, this is what I didn't dare pray for. Divine generosity I never expected to receive.

In the yellow meadow my inner self searches for the tools in the grass. I find them and begin nailing up a new plaque. My hands won't stop shaking and the plank of wood ends up crooked. It reads: *First Time Asking ME For Advice.*

I try and tear it down. I scrabble about and get splinters under my fingernails but it won't budge. I may have secretly longed for this moment, but suddenly I don't want it.

I can't do this! I can't be the person she needs.

Almost at once realisation hits. I didn't do any of this. Years ago I prayed a desperate, painfully limited, prayer, over and over. And it was God who heard, God who acted, and God who sent a brain tumour. And that brain tumour saved her, and it saved us.

And we know that in all things God works for the good of those who love him, who have been called according to his purpose... to be conformed to the image of his Son.

Where is the girl I both loved and hated with all the ferocity of childhood? Beside me is a woman, and God put her there. My inner self gets shakily to her feet. I straighten the plaque, and then erect another one directly above it. It has an arrow, and reads: *God will continue this work.*

'Jay. That's... that's a tricky question. It's one I find hard. I don't have an answer.'

'You don't?' Jay stops, actually stops, and stares.

'Of course not!' I snort, and raise my coffee cup only to bring it back down. It's completely cold now. Super-sized drinks are overrated. 'Still, it is something I've thought about. Actually, I've written a blog post on it.'

'Oh! I haven't read that one. What's it called?'

'Er, when I say written, I mean, well, it's written in my head. I haven't actually typed it yet. But... I can tell you my thoughts, if you like?'

Jay nods. My outer self begins to speak, and doesn't stop for a while. I'm excited to share my thoughts, my struggles, my convictions. I'm thrilled that someone is asking the same questions I do about life and love. I'm absolutely *over the moon* that this person is my sister.

My inner self falls to her knees among the delicate yellow flowers and cries. Lord, what will you do next?

I can't wait.

Present Day: A Conversation with Jay

TRANSCRIPT
May 23, 2021

EMILY: So Jay! Time to fill in some blanks. Hopefully the readers have just finished the memoir, where you're in hospital, you're having surgery and it's your final year of school. Then they've read the epilogue, which is suddenly eighteen months later, and you're studying occupational therapy at university… so what happened? How did you get there?

JASMINE: Well, I got there through a lot of hard work, many doctors' appointments and hospital visits, and tons of tears (probably could fill a bucket), and looads of prayers!

I found that post-discharge was probably even a bit harder than being in hospital! It was a really big adjustment, suddenly being thrown back into the real world, where I had to catch up on months of school work before returning to my final year of school in February! I had heaps of doctors' appointments during my final year of school, and a few more minor surgeries to correct and then remove the shunt placed in hospital. It was a really big year, and it really was all through God's grace that I got through this time and survived my last year of school, and got into my dream university degree.

I had so many people praying for me and supporting me. So it's not in my own strength or power I survived that year, but God's.

EMILY: I definitely remember that time being chaotic, and like you said many tears, prayers and doctors' appointments. So now, when you think of life before and after the events of this memoir, what has changed? In what way?

JASMINE: So… nothing's changed at all.

EMILY: Haha. [drily]

JASMINE: Just kidding! A lot of people say I've had a personality transplant after coming out of hospital… and I say that as well. I went from being angry a lot to being more joyful, from being messy to a neat freak, from hating any physical activity to loving the gym, from being unmotivated to loving all things productivity! Like, watching morning routine videos on Youtube is my number one hobby. Some of this has to do with the brain tumour, I am sure, but it's also bigger than that.

In the year following this memoir, when I had the time to reflect on what had just happened, by God's grace I grew to love him more and enter into a more personal relationship with him. I learnt to trust him with my life, and I have experienced the joy and peace that comes from him.

EMILY: You've definitely changed, I think, for the better… er.. [stumbles, not wanting to imply Jasmine was terrible before] … er, maybe?

JASMINE: Just maybe! [laughs]

EMILY: Yeah. A recurring theme in this memoir is looking for the good that God promises to bring out of suffering. Have you found any of that 'good', or are you still waiting on God?

JASMINE: I absolutely believe that God works all things for good. Even really, really, tough things. I have seen so much good come out of this. Some big things, and some small.

Firstly, my experiences have brought me closer to God, reminding me that this life is not all there is to live for; that God cares and has a good plan for my life even in the darkest valleys.

Working now as an occupational therapist my experiences in hospital have given me an insight into what it feels like to be a patient, stuck in hospital, with bustling health professionals coming in and out. If I myself hadn't been in this situation, I wouldn't be able to be as compassionate or understanding. Because I *know* what it's like to be in the bed, not being able to reach things on your own, being uncomfortable and not being able to do anything about it. I know what it's like, so I am able to try and make my patients lives just a little bit better by being the health professional I would have wanted.

And these are just a couple of things; not to mention I feel I've become a more understanding friend and being more grateful for the little things in life – even just being able to tidy my room for myself! Which I like to do—

EMILY: All the time! [laughs]

JASMINE: —everyday, and I am sure God will continue to use my circumstances for his good, because with him nothing is wasted.

EMILY: At the time of this conversation in 2021, it's been over five years since the events of the memoir. What's life like for you now?

JASMINE: Well, life has changed dramatically! I've moved out of home and have been an occupational therapist for a few months now, working in the same local health district as Emily was heading into just as I was heading out of hospital. Which is crazy!
I do have a lot of chronic health complications following my brain tumour, including visual field loss and an array of other conditions which require medication and monitoring, but at the moment things are stable, I am enjoying work, I love spending time with my friends and family, and so I'm very, very thankful to my heavenly Father for his blessings.

EMILY: Me too. Now, I was actually just talking to someone today about how brave I think it is of you to allow me to write this book. And when I approached you with the idea after a lot of prayer, I honestly had no idea what you'd say. I guess that was something I had to surrender to God before I wrote it. I said, God, I'm going to write this, and I'm not sure if you're going to use it in this way. So, what made you agree to let me publish our (your) story?

JASMINE: Well, to be honest it is a bit terrifying having my personal story out in the big wide world where everyone in my life can read it! But I personally love reading books like this, as you know, 'sick lit' is my favourite genre—

EMILY: Yep.

JASMINE: —I just love reading stories about sick people! Which sounds really bad, but I love it. [laughs]

EMILY: Trust me, I know. [drily]

JASMINE: And if my story can make someone think a little bit deeper about their life, or be a little more grateful to God for what they have, or trust him just an inch more, it will be so worth it.

EMILY: I agree. So if you could say one thing to the readers of this memoir, what would it be?

JASMINE: Can I say two things?

EMILY: Ooh, that's stretching it a bit, but go ahead.

JASMINE: One – Do not put your trust in your life in this world. Because things can change, tumours can grow, sad things do happen. But, if you put your trust in God, he can never be taken away from you. He is our only sure foundation.

Two – when I was in hospital, one nurse kept saying to me 'soon this will all be a distant memory'. At the time, I couldn't ever imagine it being just a distant memory… and I did try! But now it is. So remember that things do pass, nothing is forever. And, if you have your trust in Jesus, you're not going through the hard times alone. He is with you, carrying you though. This horrible time will pass, and as Christians we have the hope of something so much better in the future.

EMILY: Very true. Thanks Jay. Now, not to take the spotlight off you, but you've talked enough… joking! But do you have any questions for me?

JASMINE: Right, well, now I can relax. [sighs]

EMILY: You've still got to ask the questions.

JASMINE: Oh yeah. What was it like having your sister in hospital and being virtually helpless?

EMILY: Read the memoir. [dead-pan]

JASMINE: Wow, okay then. [laughs]

EMILY: Nah, jokes aside, it was heart-wrenching. I've never felt anything like it before, or since, actually. It physically hurt. I would have done anything, and yet there was nothing I could do. That was the worst part... you were helpless and I was helpless to help you. You were my little sister, and I wanted nothing more than to protect you against everything and anything, because, that's the point, you know? That's what a big sister does. But instead I had to surrender you to God, and that was one of the hardest things I've ever done.

JASMINE: Naw... So how did you manage to finish your final university exams during this time? 'Cause, I just can't imagine doing that... so tell us your secret!

EMILY: I have no idea! I don't even remember them. I found my transcript much later, and it tells me my marks dropped, but in God's kindness I passed everything, and it's just a blur now.

JASMINE: Alright, so not to fish for compliments or anything [laughs]… but I've mentioned how I've changed since coming out of hospital, what do you think?

EMILY: I agree with all you said, but what I didn't expect was how *you* changing would change me! I found it really hard to move from being your protector and advocate, to being your sister and companion again once you were on the road to recovery. You were my life for three months and a long time afterward, and it took time to adjust internally to the fact that you have your own life without me.
In the same way, it made me realise how much of my identity I had built on you. I think I always subconsciously compared myself to you. Because, like, I was the neat one, you were the messy one, etc. etc. Now it's the other way around, and in many other aspects as well! In changing, you changed me. It made me at first (and still makes me at times) feel a bit lost and… just a bit confused. It was so sudden. But I wouldn't have it any other way. Not only is God teaching me to build my identity solely on him, but the child who went into hospital is gone, and in her place I have a capable, mature, godly woman and friend.

JASMINE: Beautiful, you forgot beautiful.

EMILY: Oh it's not you I'm talking about [laughs]. Joking. When I think back to all my prayers for you as a teenager and young adult, I am overwhelmed by God's kindness. I once told him that all I wanted in life was you to love him completely, and that if he answered that one prayer, I would be able to die completely happy. In one sense that's still true. On the other hand, well, in answering that one prayer so spectacularly, I've been set free to pray so many more big prayers!

JASMINE: Very good…

EMILY: Touching?

JASMINE: Touching. And I also wanted to say, I'm not perfect everyone; this makes me sound like I'm an angel!

EMILY: Trust me, I know you're—

JASMINE: I'm not an angel.

EMILY: She's not an angel. [laughs]

JASMINE: So…to conclude, what was one thing you learnt from this and want to tell the readers?

EMILY: Ooh it's my turn again.

JASMINE: Yeah, I basically just re-wrote all your questions.

EMILY: I noticed. [laughs] But what do I want to say? I want to say that God actually can and does do miracles. He actually can and does intervene in our lives. Not everyone gets healed of a brain tumour, not everyone's loved one comes to know Jesus - but while we live, there is hope. I began the three months as an incurable cynic. Now, well, I'm never naturally going to be a die-hard optimist—

JASMINE: She listens to sad violin music!

EMILY: —but I like to think I'm at the very least a hopeful cynic. I choose daily to pray big prayers, to wait on God, and to dare to hope – even when it doesn't come naturally to me.
There haven't been any further miraculous healings, not as described in this memoir, but each day I see a hundred 'smaller' miracles. God can and does transform hearts and lives. He is at work. He is good.
And if that's the only thing I write until my dying breath, it will be enough.

JASMINE: Amen.

Acknowledgements

I never expected how *communal* writing a memoir would turn out to be. Writing my story became an invitation for other people to tell me theirs. The three months Jay was in hospital were *filled* with stories, and the more I hear them, the more I realise how much bigger this book could have been!

Dad's story, of juggling full-time work and driving to the hospital each night and weekend, could be a book in itself. So too, could Mum's story of fighting ill-health and blood sugar induced migraines to be at the hospital as often as possible. Jay's story, of course, could probably fill a trilogy. Then there are the stories of all who supported us, from near and far. This book doesn't do you justice, and a mere 'Thank you' seems inadequate, but it's all we have.

So thank you.

Thank you to our close friends and family, who sent gifts, shared hospital visits, helped us with practicalities, listened and prayed. Thank you to friends and family from interstate and overseas, who found inventive and generous ways to show us that we are loved.

Thank you to our church family, who arranged a week long prayer roster before Jay's final operation; who fed us with a meal roster; who organised a team to fix our garden and others who came to help with housework.

Thank you to the staff at the Children's Hospital. I'll never forget the day I came in to find several nurses sitting and crying with Jay because another surgery loomed. That level of care and kindness goes beyond the professional.

Thank you to Mum and Dad, whose determination and faith kept our family together during tragedy. Thank you to Jay for giving me permission to write this story, and sharing my conviction that such a great act of God ought to be told.

Thank you to Amelia, Berna, Cecily, Jay, Kris, Laura and Lydia – for reading the first manuscript and encouraging me to continue the journey to publication. Thank you to Anthony for your feedback in the latter stages. It was invaluable.

Thank you to Anthony Brammall (again!), Louise Gosbell and Naomi Reed for your kind words and generosity. Thank you to Jen (@jennydw) for being generous with your photography skills.

Thank you to Elizabeth Chapman at D.O.L.L Publishing for believing in this story. Without your hard work and enthusiasm this book would not be here today. Thank you for taking the risk.

Most of all, thank you to my God and Lord Jesus Christ. Thank you for answering my prayers, even the impossible ones. Thank you for being enough in the waiting, and in the rescue, and in the afterward. Before this happened I owed you everything, and now I owe you everything twice over.

About the Author

Emily is an author, radiographer, and theology student. She enjoys reading and running (sometimes simultaneously!), eating peanut butter with a spoon, and talking your ear off about anything to do with Sherlock Holmes, C. S. Lewis, or her latest read. She is the founder of CalledtoWatch.com, a website and community for the friends and family of those with chronic illnesses, and can also be found at emilyjmaurits.com. She is the author of *Thomas Clarkson: The Giant with One Idea* (2021) and won first place in the Stories of Life competition with her story, 'Confessions of a Realist,' published in *Papa's Shoes* (2019).

www.ingramcontent.com/pod-product-compliance
Lightning Source LLC
Chambersburg PA
CBHW071954290426
44109CB00018B/2015